ROUTLEDGE LIBRARY EDITIONS: INDUSTRIAL ECONOMICS

Volume 32

THE SOVIET INDUSTRIAL ENTERPRISE

THE SOVIET INDUSTRIAL ENTERPRISE

Theory and Practice

ANDREW FRERIS

Routledge
Taylor & Francis Group

LONDON AND NEW YORK

First published in 1984 by Croom Helm Ltd

This edition first published in 2018
by Routledge
2 Park Square, Milton Park, Abingdon, Oxon OX14 4RN

and by Routledge
711 Third Avenue, New York, NY 10017

Routledge is an imprint of the Taylor & Francis Group, an informa business

© 1984 A.F. Freris

British Library Cataloguing in Publication Data
A catalogue record for this book is available from the British Library

ISBN: 978-1-138-30830-5 (Set)
ISBN: 978-1-351-21102-4 (Set) (ebk)
ISBN: 978-0-8153-7392-6 (Volume 32) (hbk)
ISBN: 978-0-8153-7398-8 (Volume 32) (pbk)
ISBN: 978-1-351-24305-6 (Volume 32) (ebk)

Publisher's Note
The publisher has gone to great lengths to ensure the quality of this reprint but points out that some imperfections in the original copies may be apparent.

Disclaimer
The publisher has made every effort to trace copyright holders and would welcome correspondence from those they have been unable to trace.

THE SOVIET INDUSTRIAL ENTERPRISE

THEORY AND PRACTICE

ANDREW FRERIS

CROOM HELM
London & Sydney

©1984 A.F. Freris
Croom Helm Ltd, Provident House, Burrell Row,
Beckenham, Kent BR3 1AT
Croom Helm Australia Pty Ltd, First Floor, 139 King Street,
Sydney, NSW 2001, Australia

British Library Cataloguing in Publication Data

Freris, Andrew
    The Soviet industrial enterprise.
    1. Soviet Union – Economic policy – 1981-
    2. Soviet Union – Industries
    I. Title
    338.947   HC336.25
    ISBN 0-7099-1037-1

Printed and bound in Great Britain
by Billing & Sons Limited, Worcester.

CONTENTS

LIST OF FIGURES

LIST OF TABLES

List of Tables

To my wife Anabella

PREFACE AND ACKNOWLEDGEMENTS

This book is based on my doctoral dissertation presented at the London School of Economics in 1981. The material has been extensively revised and rewritten. Current developments in Soviet planning up to the Spring of 1983 have been included where necessary or relevant.

Most of the thesis was written under the supervision of Prof. P. Wiles and several sections from it were presented at his and Dr. S. Gomulka's seminars at LSE. Their help and advice is gratefully acknowledged especially that of Prof. Wiles. Further thanks are due to Dr. A. Zauberman for introducing me to the field of Planometrics and to my friend and colleague Dr. P. Wiedemann for his help and support over the years.

Sections of Chapter 6 were first published in the Jahrbuch der Wirtschaft Osteuropas - Yearbook of East-European Economics Band 9/II, 1981. My thanks to publishers Günter Olzog Verlag, Munich, for permission to reproduce this material.

From reading the prefaces of practically every academic book written by a married man it appears that wives bear the brunt of authorship. Mine was not an exception and this, amongst other reasons, is why the book is dedicated to her.

A.F. Freris
Department of Economics
City of London Polytechnic

INTRODUCTION

No centrally planned system can afford the collection, verification and dissemination of the volume of information necessary to control with a high degree of accuracy and certainty the behaviour of agents carrying out the instruction of the planners. It must therefore follow that the microeconomic analysis of planning is mainly concerned with the explanation of the behaviour of production units that operate within constraints, but are still able to:

(a) exercise a degree of control over how or whether to execute parts of a plan;

(b) exercise a degree of control over the quantity and type of information they pass on to planners in the process of the formation of the plan.

This book explores aspects of the behaviour of the Soviet industrial enterprise, drawing mostly on its experiences in the late 1970s and early 1980s, but also examining where necessary, the environment of its operations in the post-1965 reforms period.

The 'theory of the Soviet enterprise' is perhaps a misnomer. As Wiles points out 'an enterprise is a congeries of people'.(1) In the case of the Soviet Union the congeries is primarily interacting with its supervising Ministry via associations. In this sense the theory of the firm in the Soviet Union concerns itself not so much with the interaction between enterprises or with their customers but with that of the planners and the planned. It then follows that a key component in any explanation of the behaviour of the Soviet enterprise must contain an analysis of the compatibility of the motives and drives of those responsible for seeing that the plan is carried out and the planned. An obvious area for research would be the bonus and incentive schemes in current use in the USSR. The Soviet literature, however, does not offer much guidance as to the current state of microeconomic thinking as applied to the theory of the enterprise. In fact there is a veritable dearth of models of enterprises and only very recently some attention has been paid to the subject. There is, of course, a large volume of literature on the problems of choice and application of success indicators, but this is only one aspect of the overall behaviour of the enterprise. In a sense Soviet microeconomics has been directed towards a monistic interpretation of the operations by laying undue emphasis on the problems of bonus schemes and success indicators, and therefore bypassing the issue of the degrees of freedom available to the managers in executing their plan.

As Montias(2) has indicated, assuming a typical mode of behaviour may produce some interesting results but ultimately is a misleading exercise, if the interaction of the producing units with the rest of the decision-makers such as the central supply organs, ministries etc. is not accounted for:

> The fallacy is not in the technique of analysis but in trying to squeeze more out of these models predicated on the monistic behaviour of the 'basic decision makers' in each system than these models can contribute.

This note of caution is necessary in justifying the approach adopted here when using and interpreting the results of both western and Soviet authors in this area.(3)

One of the aims of this book is to show that complex and realistic models of the Soviet enterprise built around a neo-classical model of the firm, make a limited contribution towards understanding and predicting the behaviour of enterprises, precisely because they leave out of the picture important aspects of the interaction of the planners and the planned. The main thrust of the argument will be to direct attention to, and where possible to quantify, the role of the plan itself in conjunction with the bonus schemes, given the constraints under which the enterprises operate.

The first chapter outlines some important aspects of the system of planning, recent changes in the hierarchy of control, and the financial flows of the enterprise. The second chapter examines in detail the operations of the supply system, i.e. the Gossnab and its organs, in the context of the Soviet enterprise. It is shown there that the Gossnab and its role in the planning of the enterprise has to be considered in conjunction with taut planning - the hallmark of Soviet planning practices so far. These two chapters set the factual background against which Chapter 3 surveys and develops several analytical models of the Soviet enterprise and appraises their predictions. Chapter 4 and 5 examine then in detail two important aspects of the models outlined, namely the role of the plan itself and the concept of tautness and the role of different bonus schemes in influencing or predicting enterprise behaviour. Chapter 6 outlines in detail the material incentives scheme in use in the Soviet Union during 1980-85 in the context of the points raised in the analytical chapters and finally appraises the statistical and econometric

Introduction

evidence on the success of the incentive schemes. A short con-
cluding chapter draws all the threads of the argument together
and enumerates the findings and conclusions.
    The book will be useful to students of planned economics
in general, and USSR in particular, as it attempts to build an
analytical framework of a long-neglected area in planning - that
of the microeconomics of planning. The analysis however is
backed by a wealth of statistical and empirical illustrations
that either confirm some of the accepted views of the behaviour
of the Soviet enterprises or, in a number of cases, throws a
different or unusual light on the microeconomics of industrial
planning in the USSR.

Notes

    1. P.J.D. Wiles, Economic Institutions Compared, Basil
Blackwell, Oxford, 1977, p.63.
    2. J.M. Montias, The Structure of Economic Systems, Yale
Univ. Press, New Haven, 1966, p.232.
    3. The two works cited below are the best examples of mon-
ographs by western authors on the operations of firms in centrally planned economies. In both cases however the approach
is descriptive rather than analytical and the case of the Soviet
enterprise is not covered.
    G.R. Feiwel, The Economics of a Socialist Enterprise, A
Case Study of the Polish Firm, Praeger, New York, 1965.
    D. Granick, Enterprise Guidance in Eastern Europe, Prince-
ton Univ. Press, Princeton, 1975.
    An excellent compendium of essays on the industrial enter-
prises in planned economies appeared under the editorship of
I. Jeffries: The Industrial Enterprise in Eastern Europe, Praeger,
New York, 1981. The section on the Soviet Union written by A.
Nove (pp.29-38) is informative but mostly descriptive.

Chapter One

THE STRUCTURE AND PLANNING OF THE SOVIET INDUSTRIAL ENTERPRISE

1.1 INTRODUCTION

The following five sections will summarise the institutional
background of the Soviet industrial enterprise paying particular attention to features that may affect the formulation of
analytical models of enterprise behaviour. Some detailed information is given on the formation of obyedinenii (associations)
as they now play an important role in industrial management.
Figures are also given on the growing concentration of Soviet
industry as this feature relates to the development of the associations and has tended to diminish the degree of independence
that enterprises might have enjoyed. The planning cycle of the
enterprise and the contents of the plan are then examined paying
particular attention to financial flows and the role of profit.
This is an important area as it relates to the formulation of
incentives   funds and bonuses which constitute the main topic
of Chapter 6.
      As this book is concerned with the behaviour of the Soviet
industrial enterprise it is essential to define clearly at the
outset the exact meaning of 'industrial' and 'enterprise' in
Soviet terminology(1).
      Industry covers the following sectors in the economy:
electrical energy, oil, gas, coal, ferrous and non-ferrous met-
allurgy, chemicals and petrochemicals, machine building and
metal processing, timber, wood, paper and printing, building
materials, glass and china, light and food industry, medical
and micro-biological industry and meal and fodder. It now follows that the enterprises examined here will exclude those involved in agriculture, transport and services. Distribution is
excluded as well, except that the operation of the industrial
supply system which includes some physical distribution of goods
on a wholesale basis will be examined in Chapter 2.
      An industrial enterprise is defined as a fundamental organi-
sational unit characterised by administrative and managerial
independence. More likely than not the enterprise will be expected to run on a 'khozraschet' basis.   This means that the

4

enterprise should be able to cover the expenditures from its own funds and to make a profit. Nove(2) defines as follows the implications of khozraschet for the operations of an enterprise:

> ... (it) will cover the operating expenses out of income derived from the sale of goods and services to other enterprises or (in the case of retail establishments) to the population. Similarly it will pay for its material inputs to supplying enterprises, all at prices determined by the planning authorities; it pays amortization (depreciation) charges, also at rates determined from above. Working capital is in part provided by short-term credit obtained from the State Bank; these too are planned, and bear a low rate of interest. Wages paid to workers and employees are likewise based on officially-laid-down scales...

1.2 HIERARCHICAL STRUCTURE, PLANNING AND CENTRALIZATION

Individual enterprises come into direct contact with two types of authorities: Ministries and associations. There are now three types of ministries(3):

(a) All-Union Ministries. In 1979 there were thirty-two of these covering areas such as oil, gas, paper and machine construction. Enterprises under the auspices of these types of ministries are run directly from Moscow and are not answerable to local authorities.

(b) Union-Republican Ministries. These ministries have dual offices both in Moscow and in the appropriate republic. In 1979 there were thirty of these responsible for areas such as agriculture, coal, ferrous metals and finance.

(c) Republican Ministries. These are purely local looking after local industries in their republics.

The role of these ministries in the planning of production and supply will be examined in section 1.3 below.

The enterprise will ultimately be under the auspices and direction of the two major planning organs of the State, the Gosplan and Gossnab. The first sets out the broad national output etc. targets and ensures the consistency of the plan. The latter plans the supply system inherent in the production plan as set out by Gosplan. These two organs supervise and communicate with the ministries and occasionally directly with the enterprises. The Gossnab in particular has a complex system of territorial units and departments that interrelate closely with the enterprises. The functions of the Gosplan will be examined in greater detail in section 1.3. Gossnab operations are the subject of Chapter 2.

As from 1973 industrial enterprises have been organised at

The Structure and Planning of the Soviet Industrial Enterprise

an accelerating pace into two kinds of associations:(4)

(a) 'Proizvodstvenoe' (production), usually consisting of four enterprises.

(b) 'Promyshlennoe' (industrial), a much larger body either republican or all-union intended to replace ministerial departments (glavks).

The role of the association in the planning hierarchy is envisaged in a two, three and exceptionally four-tier structure:

All union ministry or Union republican	All-union ministry or Union republican	Union republican ministry
↓	↓	↓
Production association	All-union (or republican) industrial association	Republican ministry
↓	↓	↓
Member enterprise	Production association	Republican industrial association
	↓	↓
	Member enterprise	Production association
		↓
		Member enterprise

The role and aims of the production association have been described as:

(a) To economise on information and aid planning by treating a number of production units as a single entity as far as input allocation is concerned.

(b) To concentrate and specialise production by a process of mergers and by bringing under a single management different establishments.

(c) To encourage research and development and technological progress by bringing together scientific and research institutes with actual factories so as to accommodate applied research. Indeed in Soviet literature, associations are invariably referred to as 'production and scientific-production associations', the latter being associations whose emphasis and tasks are on applied research and technological progress.

Table 1.1 shows that although production associations did exist before 1975 their rate of growth and importance accelerated greatly, especially between 1975 and 1976.   There are no comparable aggregate data available for industrial associations except for certain industries or sectors (see for example Table 1.4).

6

TABLE 1.1 Size, growth and importance of production and scientific associations

Year	Number of production and scientific associations	Total no. of individual enterprises involved	Of which independent enterprises	Percentage of total industrial sales accounted by associations	Percentage of industrial productive personnel employed by associations
1970	608	2564	1427	6.7	6.2
1971	879	3655	2124	9.6	10.6
1972	1101	4425	2645	11.5	13.0
1973	1425	5808	3295	14.5	16.5
1974	1715	6721	3930	16.0	19.0
1975	2314	9558	4663	24.4	28.8
1976	3312	15208	6979	40.5	40.9
1977	3670	15616	7113	44.3	45.0
1978	3857	17122	7254	46.3	47.3
1979	3947	17516	7366	47.1	48.4
1980	4083	17896	7542	48.2	50.1

Source: Various issues of Narodnoe Khozyaistvo SSSR.

The Structure and Planning of the Soviet Industrial Enterprise

An independent enterprise is defined as such if it has a degree of control over its plan and its execution. This will involve the enterprise in having its own accounts of financial flows and profits, receiving its own production plan and having its own managerial team. An independent enterprise is not, in other words, a department or a section of a multiplant enterprise. The term industrial-production personnel includes not only the production workers but also ancillary, supervisory and managerial staff.

It is interesting to note that although the total number of independent industrial enterprises has been falling right through the 1970s, (1973: 48,891; 1974: 48,335; 1980: 44,172), and the number of independent enterprises belonging to associations was only about 17% of the total, they nonetheless accounted for about 48% of all the sales in 1980.

It is more than likely that the drive towards greater concentration of industrial production was one of the reasons behind the creation of associations. As Table 1.2 makes clear, concentration was taking place even before the associations received official blessing and ministries ordered to accelerate their creation in 1973. By 1979 enterprises employing more than 1,000 workers accounted for more than 70% of the value of industrial output, employed almost three-quarters of all industrial workers, utilized more than 80% of the capital funds but constituted only 17.5% of the total number of enterprises.

A similar picture emerges from Table 1.3 for a number of selected industries, the possible exception being, food processing.

It is relatively easy to conclude that the growth of associations in combination with the growth of industrial concentration in the Soviet Union will be detrimental to the degree of independence of the individual enterprises. Indeed, most observers tend now to consider the formation of associations as a move towards greater centralisation of enterprise planning(5). In some of the associations the individual enterprises have kept their independence, with the association acting only as a guide for perspective planning and development and centralising the allocation of investment resources. In other cases the individual enterprises have either lost their independence i.e. may not be individually on khozraschet or are run by the central enterprise of the association as branches ("filials") or as "firms" (i.e. groupings of small enterprise).(6)

The consequences for enterprise behaviour and the role of these institutions in modelling the Soviet enterprise are not too difficult to assess, because for example, in the case of production associations instead of looking at the enterprise one may examine the behaviour of the associations vis-a-vis the planner. Soviet economists in general expect that the reduction in the number of channels through which information flows will have beneficial effects. Given that associations were actively encouraged only in the last few years, it is not surprising that

TABLE 1.2   Concentration of industrial production by size of employment in enterprises.
(All figures as percentage of totals for industry)

Yearly average no. of workers employed in independent enterprises (excl. power stations and electricity distribution)	Number of enterprises					Global (valovaya) production					Number of workers (rabochii)*					Value of fixed capital employed				
	1960	1968	1973	1975	1979	1960	1968	1973	1975	1979	1960	1968	1973	1975	1979	1960	1968	1973	1975	1979
Up to 200	63.6	56.4	54.6	55.0	45.9	15.0	11.6	10.1	9.5	5.4	13.1	9.7	8.7	8.2	4.9	10.7	7.4	6.9	6.1	3.6
201 – 500	20.7	22.7	22.9	22.1	⌉36.6	17.3	15.5	14.0	12.3	⌉20.5	17.7	15.4	14.2	12.6	⌉20.6	13.2	11.4	11.2	9.4	⌉16.0
501 – 1000	8.6	11.0	11.3	10.9	⌋	14.9	14.2	14.4	13.1	⌋	16.0	16.3	15.3	11.5	⌋	15.2	14.9	13.2	11.5	⌋
1001 and over	7.1	9.9	11.2	12.0	17.5	52.8	57.7	61.5	65.1	74.1	53.2	58.6	61.8	65.7	74.5	60.9	66.3	68.7	73.0	80.4

SOURCE: Narodnoe Khozyaistvo SSSR for 1973, pp.244-45, for 1980 p.150 and Narod. Khoz. za 60 let p.193

*Data for 1979 are based on a slightly different classification whereby the enterprises are categorised according to the number of industrial-production personnel which includes workers (rabochii) whereas the figures up to and including 1975 are based on workers only. Comparisons however with a number of years up to 1975 where data were separated into industrial-production personnel and workers indicate that the difference that this change in base makes on the measurement of concentration is negligible. So although the data for 1979 are not strictly comparable to other years they in no way distort the trend.

TABLE 1.3   Concentration in selected industries

	No. of workers	
Percentage of enterprises with more than	1,000	3,000
Cast iron, steel and rolled metals	99	94
Machine construction*	89	68
Chemicals and resins	84	62
Cement	80	12
Light industry	58	30
Food processing	23	6

* In machine construction 20% of the enterprises employed 73% of industrial-productive personnel produced 77% of the output and used 75% of the capital funds.

Sources: (i) G.A. Egiazaryan and A.G. Omarovski (Eds.): Ekonomika sotsialisticheskoi promyshlenosti, Moscow, 1977, p.151.
(ii) V.S. Bylkovskaya and I.M.M. Razumov: Mashinostroenie, ekonomika i organizatsiya, Moscow, 1975, p.75. Neither source gives dates for the data.

there is not much evidence as to how (or by how much) they could reduce administrative costs. The formation of production associations will not necessarily involve the formation of enterprises with larger physical plant sizes. It would therefore be unreasonable to expect purely technological economies of large-scale production. On the other hand if associations encourage inter-plant specialization then there is some encouraging evidence from the Soviet shoe industry.   Multi-plant enterprise formed into associations, before the movement was officially fostered and encouraged since 1973, did operate more efficiently in terms of lower level of inventories held and greater diffusion of advanced techniques across the enterprises in the association(7).   Whether these multi-plant economies of scale will apply to the rest of the industries is still an open and very hard empirical question given the very large number of factors that influence the efficiency and cost structure of enterprises in addition to the effects of organizational changes. There was no direct empirical or statistical evidence on this point in the Soviet literature surveyed.   Whether associations will improve planning and plan consistency remains to be seen, because their interests (at least for the production associations) cannot be separated from those of their constituent enterprises.

The Structure and Planning of the Soviet Industrial Enterprise

As little has changed in the system of Soviet planning since the formation of the associations one doubts the claims of expected cost reductions.

Some fragmentary evidence has been offered on the reorganization of the light industry on all-union level in the mid-1970s. Table 1.4 shows the old and the new hierarchy of planning authorities. Under this scheme the Republican industrial association will now replace the ministerial glavk and the number of enterprises will be reduced by about 1,000. Intermediate administrative units decline from 117 to 87. It is claimed that the overall savings of cost resulting from this exercise will be about 85 million rubles of which 4.8 million are accounted by the fall in administration costs.(8) Under the new system there is considerable degree of overlapping of authorities. This is particularly true with respect to the role of the associations and ministries in the supply of inputs.

TABLE 1.4   Reorganisation of light industry

OLD SYSTEM		NEW SYSTEM	
Ministry of Light Industry (USSR) ↓	Soviet of Republican Ministries ↓	Ministry of Light Industry (USSR) ↓	Soviet of Republican Ministries ↓
3 All-union Industrial Associations	Republican Ministries of Light Industry	3 All-union Industrial Associations	Republican Ministries of Light Industry ↓
34 Glavki 28 Industrial Associations		84 Republican Industrial Associations	
52 Trusts		↓	
3000 enterprises and their production associations		2000 - 2500 enterprises and their production associations	

Source: Granatkin, Ekonomika Sotsialisticheskoi promy-shlennosti, p.40

It is important to remember that industrial and production associations did exist before 1973. A trust was an association of similar enterprises brought together for managerial purposes - usually under the auspices of the Ministerial glavki concerned.

The Structure and Planning of the Soviet Industrial Enterprise

Neither western nor Soviet sources are clear on the definition of trusts. Berliner(9) for example states:

> ... Another is the traditional form of horizontally in-
> tegrated associations called a 'trust' which is often
> used to combine a number of small plants into a single
> enterprise in such industries as woodworking and gar-
> ment manufacturing.

It seems likely however that members of a trust lost their independence whereas members of associations did not. In addition
to this associations are now being formed across all industry
whereas trusts were formed in certain sectors only.

1.3 THE PLANNING CYCLE

There are two basic types of plan that impinge directly on the
industrial enterprise: the five-year plan (FYP) separated into
its annual components and the annual plan which defines, limits
and determines the actual operation of the enterprise. Although
the annual part is, of course, a section of the five-year plan,
the latter is not meant to be operational but its aim is to set
the broad outline and direction of the path to be followed by
the enterprise. In addition to these two basic plans there are
a number of longer 'perspective' ones. For example in July 1979
the USSR announced a twenty-year long-term scientific and technical progress plan to be compiled by the Academy of Sciences
in conjunction with Gosplan. At the same time, the Gosplan was
to start a ten-year medium-term plan, the first five years of
which were to be disaggregated into individual annual plans and
the other five years specified in a more general form(10).
    The basic principles of the formation and allocation of
these two basic types of plans to the agents that will execute
them are essentially the same. So in general, targets are set by
the Gosplan which are passed on in an aggregate form to ministries
which then disaggregate them into individual plans for associations and enterprises. On the basis of these general targets,
enterprises outline their own production and input requirement
plans, pass them on to their ministry which aggregates them and
finally presents them to Gosplan.   There may well be further
iterations of the plan, when the Gosplan, upon receiving the aggregate input-output requirements plans of the enterprises,
finds that the overall macro balance of resources is likely
to meet bottlenecks, shortages or there are sectoral inconsistencies. The iteration, i.e. the exchange of plans between the
Gosplan and enterprises via the ministries will continue until
a final plan emerges.   In the case of a long-term perspective
plan the aggregation will be quite high thus necessitating few
if any iterations.   But for the five-year and annual plan the
individual enterprises via their associations or ministries
will remain actively engaged into continuous planning right
through the plan period.

12

The Structure and Planning of the Soviet Industrial Enterprise

For the five-year plan the Gosplan starts the planning process by establishing, in conjunction with the economic and political priorities, aggregate targets for a number of important commodities or group of goods. These targets are incorporated in the so-called 'control figures' for each year of the FYP. These figures are passed to the appropriate ministry or republican authority which then disaggregates them into specific tasks and sends them down to the associations and enterprises. The enterprises formulate their own plans on the basis of these control figures and specify to their supervisory authorities not only their output but also their input requirements. These are aggregated by the ministries and presented to Gosplan for overall balancing and confirmation which must be given by the USSR Council of Ministers no less than five months before the start of the next five year plan period.

The annual components of the five year plan are then used as the basis for the construction of the annual plan. It is essential to emphasize that the confirmed and agreed on figures of the five year plan are by no means unchangeable or immutable when it comes to construct the annual plan. In fact in a number of cases the FYP as a whole was not even confirmed during the first year of its (supposed) operation.

The annual planning process involves not only the production but also the supply plan of the enterprise. In other words enterprises put forward the input requirements necessary for them to fulfil their planned targets. The organs and departments of the supply planning state institution, Gossnab, take over the task of 'marrying' producing and consuming enterprises. The time scale and sequence in the mid-1970s of these two annual planning processes, the production and supply, were as follows. In the early spring of the previous year the appropriate ministry, on the basis of the control figures for the relevant year, would instruct the associations and enterprises to produce their output plans which would then be discussed and amended as necessary by the ministry. Simultaneously requests for supplies and inputs (zayavki) would be sent by enterprises to the appropriate supply department of their ministry or Gossnab. By July the output plan would have been forwarded via the ministry to the Gosplan, and the Gossnab would have issued the draft plan of distribution. In August the output plan would be with the USSR Council of Ministers and by the end of December the Gosplan would have issued the approved production plan which would then reach the enterprises by mid-January of the actual plan year. Meanwhile, on the supply side, the Gossnab would have passed down during August the plan of input allocation to the ministries, associations and enterprises. These bodies would then disaggregate the input allocation into specific requests to the appropriate supply organs which would then issue them with specific orders of shipment (naryady). On the basis of these the consumer (customer) enterprises would get in contact and finalised arrangements with their specified suppliers by November-December.

1.4 THE CONTENTS OF THE ANNUAL PLAN

The basis of the operation of the enterprise is contained in its tekhpromfinplan, i.e. the technical profits and financial plan. The eleven basic parts of the tekhpromfinplan are set out in Table 1.5. The basic planned indexes handed down to the enterprise for the eleventh FYP (1981-85) were the following:(11)

Production: Total output expressed in natural units, specific totals of goods of higher quality to total output, and goods for export. In some cases the assortment of the goods is also specified. Normed Net Production (NNP).

Labour: Rates of labour productivity and the total wages fund.

Finance: Total profit, profitability and payments to and from the budget.

Capital Construction: Capital construction including the introduction of new processes, repairs and the commissioning into operation of new productive capacity.

Technological Progress: Introduction of new technology and new products.

The rest of the planned targets and indexes such as planned costs and their reduction, the size of incentive funds etc. are set by the associations or enterprises themselves and they do not need confirmation by higher organs other than those directly above the associations.

Three observations are in order here:

Firstly, the tekhpromfinplan establishes the overall framework of the operations of the enterprise. The targets that the enterprises are expected to fulfil both through the explicit pressure of the incentives system and through the plan's own emphasis are output, (especially high quality products), labour productivity and profitability. It is true that Soviet planners frequently make what appears to be a drastic change in the framework and direction of planning. The output and productivity targets however are ever-present and important enough to allow for generalisations without undue loss of detail.

Secondly, the success of the operations of the enterprise are judged by fulfilling planned targets. The material-technical supply plan is not incorporated in the success indicators or incentive schemes.   In other words there is no reward in not breaking the input plan, except in cases such as technological progress or savings of inputs where separate bonus schemes exist.   In fact the enterprises under the system of taut planning are likely to use to the limit all the inputs allocated.

The Structure and Planning of the Soviet Industrial Enterprise

TABLE 1.5   Contents of the Tekhpromfinplan

I Basic indexes	A summary of all the basic productive-economic operations of the enterprise.
II Output and sales plan	Output and sales of industrial production. Productive capacity and its utilization.
III Plan for raising the efficiency of production	Introduction of new technology. Increases in the efficiency of use of energy, materials, fuel and labour. Introduction of automation in management and production planning.
IV Plan norms	Input utilisation norms.
V Plan of capital construction	Investment plan and utilisation of new capital.
VI Supply plan	Input use: sources and supplies.
VII Labour and wages plan	Increases in labour productivity. Balance of labour hours available. Labour intensity of production plan. Qualification and skills of labour force.
VIII Profits, profitability and cost plan	Decrease in production costs through greater efficiency. Estimation of departmental and total factory expenses. Costs of production. Depreciation deductions. Profit and profitability.
IX Plan of economic incentives fund	Material incentives fund and other bonuses.
X Finance plan	Flows of funds, credits and use of funds.
XI Plan for cultural development of the member of the enterprise	Improvements in the professional-technical qualifications of workers. Socio-cultural activities.

Source: Granatkin, Ekonomika sotsialisticheskoi promysh-
          lennosti, pp.68-69.
          G. Ya. Kiperman (Ed.) Osnovy ekonomiki i planirov-
          aniya promyshlennykh predpriyatii, Moscow 1974,
          Ch.2 passim.

In addition to this since the enterprises cannot legally obtain inputs other than those indicated in the naryad-zakaz system, breaches of the input plans either remain hidden or are authorised by the planners. Although there are financial penalties for breaking the supply plan, (i.e. fines for non-delivery, delays, breaches of assortment or quality plans) the success of the operations of the enterprise is not judged on the basis of whether it operates strictly within its supply plan. All this of course disregards the chain-reaction effects and costs of the under-fulfilment of output plans on other enterprises dependent for their inputs on the enterprise in question.

Thirdly, the majority of the targets are either self-explanatory or will be discussed in detail in later sections. One target however merits a separate mention because it does represent an innovation for the eleventh FYP compared to the previous plans.

As from 1 January 1982 a new planned target was added to those that industrial enterprises are expected to fulfil, the Normed Net Production or NNP, (normativnaya chistaya produkt-siya).(12) More than 3,200 enterprises under the auspices of thirty-four ministries are now incorporating this target in their plans. The ministries include all areas of machine construction, but in the cases of oil, gas, energy and non-ferrous metals only manufacturing enterprises are to be included. In some other ministries, such as for ferrous metals, the scheme is being introduced on an experimental basis.

The NNP is basically a form of value added; it is expressed in terms of the direct labour costs involved in the production of a good including a profit mark-up on labour costs only. Specifically, three steps are necessary to calculate NNP for any class of goods produced by enterprises.

Firstly, a ratio K is estimated using the sum total of wages paid, including deductions for social insurance, to technical, managerial and ancillary staff, divided by the total wages plus social security deductions paid to production workers only. So a $K = 2$ means that for every one rouble paid in wages to production workers, two roubles are paid to engineering, managerial etc. personnel.

Secondly, the cost of production per unit of the good in question is estimated minus any expenditures, on raw materials, semi-finished goods other inputs and energy. This 'net cost' (NC) includes the wage per unit of production workers, and preparation costs and maintenance of equipment. The 'net cost' is then multiplied by the profit mark-up margin of the enterprise to give the profit component of NNP. Call this: $\pi(NC)$.

Finally the wage cost per unit including the wages of all technical, managerial and production workers is calculated. Call the wages of production workers, W, and those of other workers W*. NNP can then be defined as

$$NNP = W + W(K) + \pi(NC) \qquad = W + W\left(\frac{W^*}{W}\right) + \pi(NC).$$

The K coefficient (i.e. the $\frac{W*}{W}$ ratio) will not be estimated individually for each enterprise neither will NC. In cases where
more than one enterprise is producing the good in question, both
these components will be calculated on the basis of branch averages.
The NNP can be used in a number of ways both as a planned
index and as a means to increase the overall economic efficiency
of enterprises. For example, setting a particular NNP target
rather than the value of output will discourage enterprises
from using expensive materials in production, a practice that
could boost the value of output without any increases in productivity. Similarly the difference between the rates of growth
of NNP and of the value of output (given its price) will reflect
increases in labout productivity. It is also hoped that NNP
will help to make meaningful comparisons in the level of wholesale prices between sectors by examining the percentage of the
wholesale prices accounted for by NNP, the remainder being an
estimate of the 'material intensity' i.e. use of non-labour inputs in production.
Given the basically experimental nature of the concept and
the fact that it has been introduced to less than 8% of the industrial enterprises, it is early yet to pass judgement on its
relative usefulness. Like all past experiments and reforms it
has to be measured against the overall planning techniques in
current use. The NNP is not the start of a radical departure
from the old and trusted methods and planned indicators but one
more attempt to increase labour productivity and the efficiency
by which non-labour inputs are used.

1.5 FINANCIAL FLOWS AND ACCOUNTS

The financial plan of the enterprise expresses in value terms
the contents of the general economic and production plans where
these are formulated in physical terms. Every physical transaction either between enterprises or enterprises and the state
is affected through bank deposits and therefore will be reflected on their financial flows. So fulfilment of the financial
plan will in some cases reflect fulfilment of the 'real plan'.
Since prices of the goods or inputs sold and purchased are in
almost all cases fixed, increases in profits or profitability,
reductions in costs of production, changes in the use of circulating capital and credit can only be achieved by changes in
productivity i.e. by changes in the use of labour and capital
equipment. The fundamental ideas of 'khozraschet' as defined in
the Introduction to this chapter are based on the use of financial flows and financial planning and are designed to foster
microeconomic efficiency in input use. Furthermore since every
physical transaction has a counterpart in financial flows, the
operations of the enterprise can be double-checked by the State
Bank (Gosbank). This is the technique of the so-called control
by the ruble whereby authorization to effect or receive payments

via bank accounts are cross-referred by the bank to its own copy
of the enterprise's plan(13).

Table 1.6 sets out in a simplified form the financial plan
of an enterprise or association. The separation of the accounts
in four sections has been kept as it follows the current Soviet
accounting practice. The whole system could, of course, have
been presented as a double-entry exercise or as a flow of funds
chart.

The rest of this section explains and discusses in some
detail the components of the financial plan and flows of enterprises and sets them in the context of their operations and objectives as expressed in the general economic plan. Reference
is made by number to the entries in Table 1.6.

Given the key role that profits play in the financial plan
of the enterprise, it is appropriate to start with the definition
of profits, profitability and particularly that of prices used
to determine the value of sales and hence to arrive at gross
profits.

The wholesale price used for the derivation of profits
consists of the costs of production plus a profit mark-up. The
profit margin is determined along the following lines(14):

$$P^* = \frac{K\pi}{TC}$$

where P^* is the profit margin as a percentage of cost, K is the
average amount of fixed and circulating capital used by the enterprise, π is a profit norm set by the authorities (now on the
average 15%, but see below) and TC are the total costs of production. So, for example, the price of any single good α is
defined as (subscripts denote the good in question):

$$P_\alpha = C_\alpha + \frac{P^* C_\alpha}{100} = C_\alpha + \frac{\frac{K}{TC} C_\alpha}{100}$$

If the enterprise is producing a variety of goods, TC will
denots the total costs of production including the costs of
producing goods α, and C_α will denote the average cost of producing α.

After the 1966-67 price reforms the π component is now
differentiated amongst sectors so although on the average π is
set at 15% it may vary. It now stands at 37.8% for light industry and 18.9% in food processing. The following reasons
have been advanced for the differentials in profit margins:

(a) A deliberate act of policy designed to keep the prices of
certain products relatively lower in comparison to other
similar goods. For example since 1967 the profit margins
on agrotechnical equipment were set lower to those on general machine tool construction. The aim presumably was to
subsidize agricultural investment.

TABLE 1.6   Finance plan of industrial enterprises

A Receipts and Income	B Payments and deductions	C Credits	D Budgetary provisions
1 Turnover tax	5 Centralised capital investment provisions	10 Net long-term credits for capital investment	12 Payments for the use of production funds (i.e. fixed and circulating capital)
2 Profit [defined as receipts from sales at wholesale prices, (i.e. excluding turnover tax) - labour and material costs - depreciation]	6 Increases of own circulating capital	11 Net loans for decentralised investment projects	13 Fixed rental payments
	7 Payments for capital repairs and renovations		14 Payment to the budget of the profit remainder
3 Depreciation allowances (for replacement and renovation)	8 Deductions from profit to; a. Material Incentives Fund. b. Development of Production Fund c. Socio-cultural and housing fund		15 Turnover tax
4 Receipts from the Development of Production Fund and other decentralised sources of investment funds	9 Provisions for depreciation that will be added to the Development of Production Fund		

Source: See   Footnote (13).

Note: This is a simplified version of accounts in the sense that the same item may appear both as a receipt and as a payment. For example, turnover tax is both a receipt for the enterprise but is, of course, paid back to the state budget.   Centralised   investment   expenditures   appear   simultaneously   as   a payment from the budget as an expenditure by the enterprise. It therefore follows that cols. A+C=B+D.

(b) To encourage technological progress.(15)

Differences in labour and capital intensity between sectors are allowed for because profitability is now expressed as a percentage on capital, and enterprises since 1965 have to pay a 6% charge on capital used. The charge is not regarded as a cost of production but a payment out of earned profits. It then follows that the planners have to ensure that enterprises would end up with revenues high enough to allow them to pay that charge with a 'reasonable' amount left over for all the ordinary profit retentions. As Berliner indicated:

> Industries that use large quantities of capital relative to total costs require a larger excess of revenues over costs to pay their capital charges than industries that use less capital. The former are therefore assigned larger profit mark-ups than the latter in pricing their products.
>
> (The Innovation Decision in Soviet Industry p.243)

It is interesting to note that under this mark-up scheme if K increases, ceteris paribus, the gross profit margin would also increase. Whether, however, this would benefit the enterprise would depend on:

(a) The behaviour of average costs (AC).   Defining profitability, R, as

$$R = \frac{\text{Profit margin} \times \text{Output sold}}{\text{capital employed}} = \frac{K\pi}{TC} \, Q/K$$

(where Q stands for output sold in physical terms)

then $R = \pi \frac{Q}{TC}$ or $\pi \frac{1}{AC}$

(b) The definition of profitability used. If net profitability is used which includes payments for capital utilized then the deductions from profits of these payments will effectively decrease the profit margin.

It is precisely these points that make the analysis of profits and profitability complex in the case of multi-product enterprises where different goods bear different proportions of the total costs of production. What is important to note here is that capital intensive techniques of production are unlikely to benefit the enterprise profit-wise unless they lead to a fall in the average cost of production proportionally higher than the increase in interest rate and payments for the use of capital.(16)

Profits as defined in A2 in Table 1.6, do not include the charges made for using capital (plata za fondi). Profitability, however, is defined as the ratio of profits to the total fixed and normed circulating capital. The definition of gross profitability (balansovaya rentabel'nost') does not allow for deductions from profits for payments made for using capital, fixed rental payments and interest charges on loans and credit. In calculating net profitability (raschetnaya rentabel'nost') all these payments and charges are deducted from profits.   In cases where net profitability is used, the fixed capital in the denominator of the expression includes only the capital funds on which the enterprise pays charges or interest rates.   It would exclude, for example, capital financed from the enterprise's own Development and Production Fund.(17)

Item A3, depreciation depends on the centrally authorised norms. For example, 3.4% per annum is allowed for buildings, 13.5% for transport equipment and so on. As will be shown later on, depreciation allowance is a source of funds for decentralised investment.(18)

Item B8a, the Material Incentives Fund (MIF), is examined separately and in great detail in Chapter 6. Suffice to indicate now that it is formed from profits on the condition that key planned indications are fulfilled, and is used for the payments of bonuses to managers and workers.

The Development of Production Fund, B8b, is meant to be an additional source to centralised financing of new technology in the enterprise, and the mechanization, renovation and modernization of existing equipment and processes.(19)

The DPF is formed from:

(a)   Deduction from profit and the depreciation funds set aside by the enterprise. The norms of deduction from both these sources are set by the supervising ministry. The total sums set aside can be increased (or decreased) depending on whether the planned profit and planned depreciation funds turn out to be smaller (or bigger) than the actual, realised ones. In the case where the profit plan is not fulfilled the PDF cannot decline to less than 40% of its planned size, i.e. the amount foreseen in the plan at the start of the year.

(b)   A share in the profits made by selling high quality goods.

(c)   Fees received by hiring out to other enterprises the scientific and technical services of the enterprise.

The significance of the DPF will be re-appraised presently when the size and sources of decentralized investment are examined.

The Socio-cultural and Housing Fund (SCHF) in B8c is formed out of profit except that it is expressed as a percentage (30% to 50%) of the Material Incentives Fund. It therefore follows that it increases or decreases according to the degree of plan fulfilment as reflected on MIF itself. The actual size of the coefficient used, i.e. whether 30% or up to 50% of MIF is determined by the social needs of the enterprise involved, i.e. the state of the housing stock, the number of young children in the workers' families etc. The fund is used for the construction and repair of housing, clubs, recreational facilities for adults and children, canteens and the financing of holidays, stays at sanatoria etc.

Items D12 cover payments for the amount of both fixed and circulating capital funds used by the enterprise. The normed circulating capital is determined on the basis of the estimates of daily expenditures on materials multiplied by norms indicating the length in days of each production cycle. The estimates of the expenditures on materials are based on the norms of input utilization per unit of output. These are examined in greater detail in Chapter 2 in this book. The value of circulating capital excludes any credit used to finance it; similarly in estimating the value of fixed fund in most cases no allowance is made for depreciation but the value arrived at excludes again credit used to finance these capital funds. The rate currently charged is 6%; there are however special provisions for low profit or loss making enterprises and for certain types of organizations. In those cases rates can vary from 2 - 6% or waived altogether.(20)

Fixed rental payments, D13 are levied on enterprises particularly favoured by geography, location, geomorphology, etc. thus resulting to above average profitability. The payments are determined on an ad hoc basis depending on individual circumstances.

D14 is simply the residual of the actual (as opposed to planned) profit after all deductions have been made. This is then returned to the state. In the case of a negative residual (losses) the state makes a payment to the enterprise.

1.6 THE ROLE OF PROFITS AND INVESTMENT

It is by now apparent that profits are the linchpin of the financial plan as they are the main source for both centralised and decentralised investment and for the incentive funds. Table 1.7 shows how profits of industrial enterprises were allocated to various uses.

The largest single item in this allocation is the residual profit surrendered back to the state. Incentive funds claim about 17% of the total profits. The major source of investment funds for the enterprise is, of course, the centrally allocated ones. Table 1.8 gives some idea of the magnitude involved, and taken in conjunction with the data of Table 1.9, confirms the importance of budgetary appropriations, i.e. the centralised financing of investments. It is important to note however that as all funds for the financing of fixed capital formation in industry, transport, communication, trade, education, health and recreational facilities, construction and municipal housing as well as research facilities have to be channelled through the Investment Bank, the data in Table 1.8 do not refer exclusively to industry. The source did not provide disaggregated sectoral data.

TABLE 1.7   Allocation of profits of industrial enterprises   (Figures as percentage of total)

	1972	1973	1974	1975	1976	1977	1978	1979	1980
Payment to Budget of which:	61	57	57	58	59	61	59	60	60
(a) Direct deductions	2	2	1	1	1	1	1	1	1
(b) Payments for fixed and circulating capital	19	20	20	22	23	23	23	23	23
(c) Rental (fixed) payments	4	5	5	4	4	3	2	1	1
(d) Surrender of residual profit	35	30	30	30	30	33	32	34	34
(e) Unaccounted for*	1	-	1	1	1	1	1	1	1
Remaining at the disposal of the enterprise, of which:	39	43	43	42	41	39	41	40	40
(a) Used for capital investment	13	12	13	10	11	5	4	4	4
(b) To incentive funds	16	16	16	17	16	17	18	17	17
(c) Other**	10	15	14	15	14	17	19	19	19

Source: Various issues of Narodnoe Khozyaistvo SSSR

* The percentages do not add up. There is a small discrepancy due to some deductions not appearing in the statistics.

** Directed towards increasing own circulating funds, covering planned losses, repaying bank debts and interest payments etc.

TABLE 1.8   Sources of financing centralised fixed investment
distributed by the investment bank

(billions of rubles)

	1959		1966	
	Amount	% of total	Amount	% of total
Resources of enterprises:				
Depreciation allowances	2.8	14.9	7.9	27.9
Profits	2.5	13.4	3.0	10.5
Other	0.4	1.9	1.0	3.7
Total	5.7	30.2	11.9	42.1
Budgetary appropriations	13.2	69.8	16.4	57.9
Grand total	19.0	100	28.4	100

Source: Garvy, Money, Financial Flows and Credit in the Soviet
Union, pp.69-70. Figures are rounded up.

TABLE 1.9   Sources of funds for centralised investment 1972-74
for the national economy (% of total)

	1972	1973	1974
Budget sources	47.1	47.8	47.8
Profits	19.4	16.1	16.8
Depreciation	21.6	23.0	21.8
Long-term bank credit	2.6	3.3	3.5
Other	9.3	9.8	10.1

Source: P.N. Zhevtyak and V.I. Kolesnikov: Pribyl'v sotsiali-
sticheskom rasshirennom vosproizvodstve, Moscow, 1976,
p.154.

Note   The source does not specify whether agriculture or transport are included.

A study covering data from twenty-three industrial ministries (both All-Union and a few belonging to RSFSR) found that budgetary sources covered 35.4% of investment expenditures in 1970, 33.8% in 1972 and 34.6% in 1973. Significantly, however, there were very wide differences between ministries and between different years for the same ministries that made these averages a rather rough guide.(21)

A roughly similar picture emerges from Table 1.10 except the role of depreciation is comparatively larger. This might be due to the fact that the coverage of Table 1.10 is exclusively industrial whereas in the other tables it is not. The dramatic fall in the role of budgetary sources between 1969-70 is partially explained by the fact that the Ministries can direct enterprises to channel profits into particular projects as well as appropriating them only to refund them in the form of direct grants. Similarly, funds set aside for depreciation are either surrendered to the relevant Ministry or are directed towards decentrally financed investment. Since the major inputs for industrial investment have to be planned by Gosplan and distributed by Gossnab it is important to emphasise that the discussion here concerns decentrally (or centrally) financed investment rather than decentralised decision-making on investment.

TABLE 1.10   Sources of financing centralised capital construction in industry and sub-departments of some ministries in the Ukraine. All figures as % of total

Year	Source of finance			
	Budget	Profits of Enterprises	Depre-ciation	Other
1966	38.2	17.8	39.7	4.3
1967	36.7	19.0	40.5	3.8
1968	38.4	20.7	37.7	3.2
1969	40.2	19.4	37.3	3.1
1970	23.1	28.0	43.8	5.1
1971	25.4	21.9	37.4	15.3
1972	26.1	24.8	33.2	15.9
1961-65	53.3	9.7	24.9	12.0
1966-70	34.9	20.9	29.6	4.6

Source: L.A. Ol'shevskaya, Sovershenstvovanie kreditovaniya promyshlennogo proizvodstva, Kiev 1976, p.46.

The Structure and Planning of the Soviet Industrial Enterprise

The picture for industry can be considerably clarified by combining several sets of figures from the data in the annual statistical yearbook. The unimportance of decentrally financed investment for the industrial sector can then be confirmed. Table 1.11 sets out the results. It is clear that decentralised investment (mainly via the DPF) accounts for about 14% of the total industrial investment carried out. It is also interesting to note that the amount of profits centrally directed and set aside for investment has been falling, its place being taken over by direct grants, and marginally only, by DPF. This can also be seen from the data in Table 1.7 where the percentage of profit used for investment by the enterprise fell rapidly after 1976. It is important to emphasise again that the discussion here concerns centrally or decentrally financed investment rather than the decision whether to invest at all. Even so, any movement away from financing investment from sources of funds generated by the enterprises can only diminish even further their degree of independence. The position of the planners will be strengthened in that they not only decide whether to invest or not but they also provide the funds.

The role of the bank credit (both short and long) is very small and is, of course, subject to direct central controls and hence does not play any significant role in the investment decision.

A few final comments can now be made concerning the material presented. The amount of profits that enterprises make depends not only on costs but also on the capital structure. The profit left at the disposal of enterprises have not changed greatly since the mid-1970s but still remains well less than 50% of the total made. Investment is under the total control of the Central authorities; decentralised investment here means decentrally funded. Capital equipment, plant etc. has still to be obtained from the Gosplan and distributed by the Gossnab. The degree of central control as seen from the individual enterprise's point of view has increased with the creation of associations and the ever-present rise in industrial concentration.

There is no contradiction involved in claiming that profits are important in influencing enterprise decisions as they are the major source of incentives funds, but at the same time point out that both the planning and financing of investment is firmly within the hold of the planners. It is a fundamental premise of this book that enterprises in the Soviet Union do exercise a degree of control over the formation and execution of their plans notwithstanding the degree of centralisation of investment decision. Profits are an important variable in the decision-making of the enterprise because they are part of the plan and also because they are the main source of bonuses.

TABLE 1.11   Sources of investment funds in industry

Year	I Total capital investment in industry only (ml. rubles)	II Total profits in industry (ml. rubles)	III Total profit used for capital investment (ml. rubles)	IV Column III as a % of I	V Funds from the Production Development Fund as a % of Column I
1972	32,400	59,397	7,721	23	12.5
1973	34,112	60,042	7,205	21	11.3
1974	36,700	64,223	8,348	22	10.6
1975	38,932	65,941	6,594	16	13.8
1976	40,790	64,827	5,834	14	14.6
1977	42,563	67,161	3,358	7.8	14.5
1978	45,240	70,659	2,826	6	14.7
1979	43,360	70,346	2,813	6	14.0
1980	46,505	73,295	2,921	6	15.6

Source: Various issues of Narodnoe Khozyaistvo SSSR.

Note: The total profits set aside for investment do not include the part of profits allocated to the Development of Production Fund. This is so because Soviet statistics include the part of profits set aside for DPF under the heading of 'Incentive Funds' (see Table 1.7). So column V in this table is free of any double-counting when compared with column IV. The Tipovaya Metodika is also clear on this point because it describes profits as one of the sources for centralised investment and the DPF as a source for decentralised investment.

Notes

1. M.G. Nazarov (Ed.), Sotsial'no-ekonomicheskaya stat-istika-slovar', Moscow 1981, p.56 and p.70.
2. A. Nove, The Soviet Economic System, G. Allen & Unwin, London 1977, pp.28-29.
3. S. Sh. Zamaleev (Ed.), Ekonomika otraslei narodnogo khozyaistva, Kiev 1976, pp.46-49 and also P.R. Gregory and R.C. Stewart, Soviet Economic Structure and Performance, 2nd edition, Harper & Row, New York 1981, pp.116-120.
4. Yu. A. Granatkin, Ekonomika sotsialisticheskoi promy-shlennosti, Leningrad 1975, pp.30-35.
5. A.C. Gorlin, 'The Soviet Economic Associations', Soviet Studies, Vol.26, No.1, January 1974, pp.3-27.
6. Granatkin, Ekonomika sotsialisticheskoi promyshlen-nosti, pp.31-33.
7. Gorlin, 'The Soviet Economic Associations', pp.14-23.
8. Granatkin, Ekonomika sotsialisticheskoi promyshlen-nosti, p.41.
9. J.S. Berliner, The Innovation Decision in Soviet Industry, MIT Press, Massachusetts 1976, p.129.
10. The material on the planning process in the next paragraphs draws from:
(a) Ekonomicheskaya Gazeta, No.32, August 1979. This issue contained the text of the July 1979 decree which set out measures for 'the improvement of planning and intensification of the influence of economic mechanism on the effectiveness of production and quality of labour'. This decree will be referred to from now on as the July 1979 measures.
(b) M. Ellman, Socialist Planning, Cambridge University Press, Cambridge 1979, pp.20-29.
(c) M. Cave, Computers and Economic Planning: The Soviet Experience, Cambridge University Press, London 1980, pp.32-35.
11. For the eleventh FYP (1981-85) see the July 1979 measures. In general, with the exception of the Normed Net Production, the planned targets for the eleventh FYP were almost identical to those for the tenth FYP (1976-80). The discussion in this section draws heavily from Tipovaya metodika razrabotki pyatiletnego plana proizvodstvennogo obyedineniya (kombinata) predpriyatiya, Gosplan SSSR, Moscow 1975, which although it deals with the tenth FYP is broadly applicable to the eleventh FYP as well.
12. See the relevant announcements in Ekonomicheskaya Gazeta No.4, Oct. 1979 and No.32 Aug. 1981. Also L. Rozenova, 'Normativnaya, chistaya produktsiya i povyshenie effektivnosti proizvodstva' in Voprosy Ekonomiki No.1 1982, pp.23-32.
13. The following sections draw heavily from D.S. Molyakova (Ed.): Financy predpriyatii i otraslei narodnokhozyaistva, Moscow 1976, pp.118-129 and A.D. Millioushchikov, Raschety c byudzhetom po platezham iz pribyli, Moscow 1976, passim. See also G. Garvy, Money, Financial Flows, and Credit in the Soviet

Union, Ballinger, Massachusetts 1977, Chs. 3 and 5, and B. Horwitz, Accounting Controls and the Soviet Economic Reform of 1966, Studies in Accounting Research No.4, American Accounting Association, 1970, Ch.3.

14. L.M. Kantor (Ed.), Teoriya i metodologiya planogo tsenoobrazovaniya, Moscow 1976, Ch.XI, esp. p.200.   See also Ekonomicheskaya Gazeta No.21, May 1980.

15. Kantor, Teoriya ... , pp.187-88.

16. This section on pricing and profit mark-up covers the cases of established goods only. The very important but complex problems of the pricing of new goods and the treatment of technological innovation is examined extensively in Berliner, The Innovation Decision in Soviet Industry, Part II passim.

17. Kiperman, Osnovy ekonomiki ..., p.183.

18. Tipovaya Metodika, p.159.

19. Ekonomicheskaya Gazeta, No.18, April 1980 published an official decree on the formation of the DPF for the eleventh FYP. See also some additional details in Berliner, The Innovation Decision ..., p.184 and Granatkin, Ekonomika sotsialisticheskoi ..., p.142.

20. For details see Ekonomicheskaya Gazeta, No.20, May 1980.

21. M. Pessel', Kredit kak faktor intensifikatsii kapital'nogo stroitel'stva, Planovoe Khozaistvo, No.1, 1977, p.51.

Chapter Two

GOSSNAB AND THE INDUSTRIAL SUPPLY SYSTEM

2.1 INTRODUCTION

The counterpart of the planning of output, financial targets
etc., which was examined in Chapter 1, is the planning of inputs.
As will emerge later on it is unrealistic to attempt to examine
these two aspects of planning separately. In the Soviet Union
however the existence of a large and elaborate set of institutions specifically designed to carry out supply planning makes
it easier to approach this area both from an institutional and
analytical point of view.

The aims of this chapter are, firstly, to outline the institutional framework of supply planning and trace the inter-
relationship with output planning; secondly, to examine the
relationship between supply planners and enterprises and finally
to examine the planning of supply organs, their targets and incentive schemes. The last part of this chapter also attempts
to integrate the function of planners as 'suppliers' to that of
enterprises as 'producers and suppliers' and hence weave it
into the main theme of this work, namely the behaviour of the
Soviet enterprise.

2.2 INSTITUTIONS OF THE SUPPLY SYSTEM

The Soviet system of planning industrial supply is separated
into those institutions directly linked to and subordinate to
the Gossnab and those related to ministries, either All-Union
or republican. In addition to this the Gossnab system itself
is further subdivided into territorial units and organs.

The centralised, Gossnab, system consists of(1):

(a) The Gossnab itself as an umbrella institution. Its overall
     function is to draft and follow up the execution of the
     material technical supply, to coordinate and balance de-
     mand for and supply of goods and inputs, to plan and exe-
     cute the assortment plan of goods according to the agreed

nomenclature, to oversee the development of wholesale trade and, finally, to oversee and direct the supplying functions of its territorial units and those of the related ministries.

(b) All-Union Main Administrations for Supply (Soyuzglavsnab-sbyty). These are concerned with the planning of the supply of specific goods, and duplicate on a broad disaggregate basis the functions of the Gossnab as described in (a). In 1974 there were twenty-five of these Administrations covering goods such as metals, chemicals etc. The emphasis of the role of these organs is on their coordinating function especially between the ministries involved both All-Union or republican. For example the electrical goods Administration coordinates the sale and supply of goods produced by forty-seven ministries, and that of metal of thirty-five different ministries(2).

(c) Main Administrations of Material Technical Supply in all the Soviet republics except RSFSR (from here on referred to by their cyrillic initials GUMTS). In 1974 there were fourteen of these; their function is to coordinate and further disaggregate the supply plan within republics in conjunction with the relevant republican ministies or with the Gossnab itself. An additional important task they execute is the formulation of the inter-regional and inter-sectoral supply plan(3).

(d) All-Union Main Administration for Equipment Supply and Construction: in 1974 there were twelve of these bodies whose task is to oversee the technical and mechanical equipping (or re-equipping) of enterprises. Their function and operation is separate from that of the actual building and construction of plant. There is a separate section in the overall output and supply plan that deals specifically with the supply of machines etc. to newly constructed enterprises or those being modernised and re-equipped:

> The most important construction projects are equipped with plant and machinery, fittings, instruments, automated and communications systems, cables and other manufactured goods by the All-Union central equipment organizations under the Gossnab and by the regional equipment organizations within the central and regional material and technical supply department. With respect to the construction projects for which they are providing equipment the All-Union equipment organizations act as holders of the plant and machinery being allocated. In the allocation plants prepared by the Gosplan and the Soyuzglavsna-bsbyty attached to Gossnab the plant and machinery for equipping construction projects are marked as a separate entry.(4)

(e)   Territorial Administrations of Material-Technical Supply
      (cyrillic initials UMTS). These are specific to the RSFSR
      which has thirty-one and to the Ukraine and Kazakh SSRs
      which have seven each.   The UMTS of RSFSR are directly
      subordinate to the Gossnab itself; those of the Kazakh
      and Ukraine to their republican authorities. The functions
      of UMTS are
      (i) to organize the supply to and from their 'rayons'
           (districts)
      (ii) to plan in greater detail the dispatch of supplies
           from supplying enterprises within their 'rayons'
      (iii) to disaggregate the supply plan of scientific
           goods within the area of their authority.
      In addition to this the UMTS plan the allocation of decen-
      trally allocated inputs.
(f)   In addition to these Administrations etc. there are GUMTS
      for each republic responsible for the allocation of oil
      and also a series of depots and wholesale centres and
      distribution points (baz, sklad, etc.) attached to the
      regional-territorial organs of the Gossnab.

    The supply system not directly related to or subordinate
to the Gossnab consists of the various Ministerial departments,
(glavks), which carry out supply planning.   Enterprises and
associations (especially All-Union industrial associations)
have their own supply sections to coordinate both the purchase
and sale of their inputs.
    A simplified picture of the hierarchical linking of these
bodies is shown in Figure 2.1.   The quantitative significance
of these bodies in the total circulation of goods (tovarooborot)
as shown in Table 2.1. It is interesting to note in that table
the relative unimportance of the ministerial supply organs
compared to the Gossnab system and its territorial bodies.

TABLE 2.1   Supply organs and commodity circulation in 1971

Organs	% of total commodity circulation	% of workers employed in the supply system
Gossnab	48.2	24.9
Oil BUMTS	9.6	22.4
Union Ministries and their glavks	14.4	10.6
Republican Ministries	14.9	3.6
Others	12.9	38.5

Source: Kurotchenko: Material'no-tekhnicheskoe snabzhenie v
          novykh usloviyakh khozyaistvovaniya, Moscow 1975, p.13.

FIGURE 2.1
Supply planning and the
Gossnab system

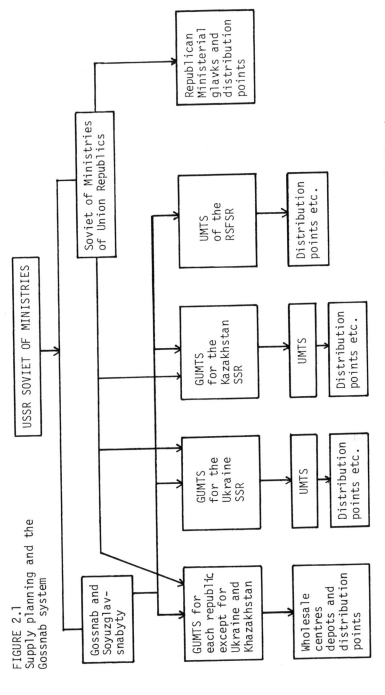

Source: Based on tables in Smirnov, Organizatsiya i planirovanie ... pp.37-39 and
         Zamaleev, Ekonomika otraslei ... p.303.

33

Gossnab and the Industrial Supply System

In appraising the role of the Gossnab it is important to keep in mind that it invariably acts as an adjunct planner to Gosplan, in exactly the same way that the Gosplan also duplicates to a limited extent the functions of the Gossnab. In deciding the vector of final demand of goods to be produced, the Gosplan, in association with the Gossnab, also decides on the allocation of certain goods. So there is a degree of overlap in the functions of the two bodies in the sense that although the primary function of the Gossnab is to execute the supply plan inherent in the output plan prepared by the Gosplan, the Gosplan also participates in some instances in deciding which producing sector receives what inputs. As has been shown in Section 1.3 there are effectively two plans in existence in the Soviet Union at any given time. The Gosplan version concerning output and the Gossnab version on inputs. Ideally the two should be consistent. Seen from the point of view of the enterprise, there is one plan concerning its own output and its destination and another for inputs. C. Krylov(5) summarised the situation thus:

> ... The plan-requisition is coordinated and compiled in Gossnab, USSR. At this point it becomes a supply-funds plan; or, to put it differently, it becomes an actual production plan for output in which production and resources are organically joined, although this balanced relationship is far from perfect. The supply-funds plan, although important, is not confirmed by higher-ranking USSR stage organs, nor does it become law ... The substantiation of both versions of the plan, the Gossnab version and the Gosplan version are about the same. Not only are both unscientific, but both are poorly founded statistically. Nonetheless, the Gosplan version becomes a law that must be carried out and adhered to. The Gossnab version is much better balanced in resources production. The demand that these plans concur, shifts the final decision to the executors ...

The potential inconsistencies in the input and output plans explains the defensive behaviour of ministries and enterprises in attempting to secure low output but high input plans thus ensuring a greater probability in fulfilling their targets. This particular aspect of supply planning is examined in greater detail in Chapter 4.

It should now be clear that in bringing user and producers of goods together the Gossnab is directly involved in planning output because:

(a) it has to plan, arrange and oversee the execution of the assortment plan;
(b) it has to plan the production and allocation of all

34

inputs, goods etc., that are not allocated by the Gosplan (funded goods) or the ministries (decentrally allocated goods).

The existence of 'dual subordination' is of course nothing new or unusual in the Soviet experience. What is not emphasised, however, in the literature is that in executing the supply plan inherent in the plan of the Gosplan, the Gossnab will have to disaggregate and therefore get involved in the detailed planning of output that will be used as inputs.

The centrally distributed products are those planned and allocated by Gosplan, Gossnab and some ministries. Some of these commodities, the funded goods, have to be allocated according to plans approved by the Council of Ministers. The decentrally distributed commodities are those whose allocation is undertaken by the territorial organs of the Gossnab and of the departments (glavki) of ministries. The number of funded commodities whose planning and allocation are undertaken by the Gosplan has fallen significantly in the post-war period from 2,390 in 1953, to 892 in 1957, 373 in 1963, 377 in 1966 and 327 in 1968. For the tenth FYP (1976-80) the number was 234 and for the eleventh FYP (1981-86) it increased to 410(6).

Given the 'dual function' of the Gossnab as the planner of supplies as well as an adjunct planner to Gosplan, it is interesting to note that during the eleventh FYP, Gossnab is scheduled to plan the balance and distribution of 300 goods not included in the list of those goods planned by the Gosplan. This represents quite a considerable increase over the tenth FYP when Gossnab balanced the production and supply of about 100 goods(7). Although these are not strictly speaking funded goods, they are neither decentrally allocated. Table 2.2 shows how the number of centrally and decentrally planned and allocated commodities has changed over time. The trend towards diminishing the number of funded goods appears to have been reversed during the eleventh FYP.

The very large discrepancy in the figures for Ministries for 1973 in Table 2.2 arises possibly because Berliner does not include all the goods which are decentrally planned and allocated. Neither source referring to 1973 specifies this particular category of goods in any detail. In fact Berliner comments that

We do not know what proportion of total industrial output is covered by those 16,000 commodities (i.e. the summation of the 1968 column, AFF) but they include all industrial materials, fuels, and equipment of any significance. The only industrial commodities that appear to be excluded are those produced locally for local use, which may be purchased by what is called de-centralized procurement. (The Innovation Decision ... p.64)

With reference to the 40,000 for 1973 commodities Kurotchenko

TABLE 2.2   Allocation of goods by planning bodies

Organ	Number of goods planned and allocated				
	1965	1968	1973	Tenth FYP 1976-80	Eleventh FYP 1981-85
USSR Council of Ministries via Gosplan (funded goods)	370	350 - 400	275	234	410
Gosplan	1538	1569	1633	2000	+2000
Gossnab and soyuzglavsnasbyty (including those via territorial organs)	18530 / NA	3301 } 12529 / 9228	6518 } 12018 / 5500	} NA	} NA
Ministries and departments	NA	1814	40000		

Sources: Data for 1965 and 1973 Kurotchenko, Material'no-tekhnicheskoe ..., p.82, data for 1968 Berliner, The Innovation Decision in Soviet Industry, p.64, tenth and eleventh FYP Chistyakov, Metodicheskie ukazaniya ..., p.113, Ekonomicheskaya Gazeta No.41, Oct. 1979.

also points out on p.83 that the ministries and departments
include sale organs which distribute internally and to other
ministries their own production.   It is therefore most likely
that Berliner's data do exclude a number of decentrally allocated and distributed commodities.
    The commodities whose supply and allocation is planned by
Ministries are those which are produced and used primarily by
enterprises under the Ministry's control or which are of low
order of priority.   Ministries however do retain an important
function in the supply systems both as 'allocation centres'
(fondoderzhateli) for funded commodities allocated by the Gosplan and for executing by disaggregation the supply plan passed
on to them.
    The process of the formation of the five year plan and its
breakdown into annual components has already been discussed in
Chapter 1 section 1.3 of this book. Here we shall concentrate
on some lesser known aspects of the supply plan of the enter-
prise(8).
    The basis of the allocation of inputs as viewed by the
'consumer' enterprise can be seen in a highly schematic fashion
on a triangular relationship in Figure 2.2.

Figure 2.2   Supply plan and the enterprise

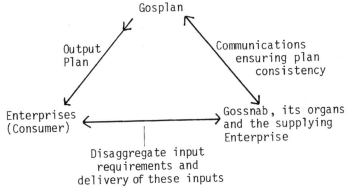

For a good allocated centrally (i.e. via Gosplan-Gossnab
system, as opposed through ministerial organs) the planning
procedure for its supply is roughly as follows. Having received
the production plan the enterprise submits its input requirement
to its administrative superior.   The norms of utilisation of
inputs are usually expressed per unit of output to be produced.
Some of the norms are established centrally and some are subject
to negotiation between the enterprise and its superiors.   The

enterprises are further constrained by the requirement that norms put forward for time period t cannot be bigger than the actual input utilisation in $t-1$. Comparisons are made between normed and actual uses and adjustments are made in the cases of deficits or surpluses. There are basically six groups of norms of input utilisation(9).

(a) Norms of the utilisation of labour hours per unit of output over the sum total of labour hours available (the 'labour budget').
(b) Norms of the utilisation of machines, instruments and equipment.
(c) Norms of the utilisation of raw materials, fuel and energy.
(d) Organisational norms of the production process and, specifically, the length of the production cycle.
(e) Financial norms with respect to the utilisation of circulating capital and the financial flows of the enterprise.
(f) Norms of the material-technical supply circuit, i.e. the costs of handling inputs.

For a good planned by the Gosplan the supervisory organs of the enterprise, a ministerial glavk will aggregate the input requirements into indents (zayavki) and these will be sent to the appropriate department of Gosplan. There the indents will be checked against the overall production plan and a distribution will be worked out. The distribution plan is a detailed version of the requirements (inputs) side of material. If no adjustments are necessary the supply side of the system then takes over in that the central and territorial organs of the Gossnab will bring consumers and supplier together by the issuing of naryad and naryad-zakaz (allocation certificates and orders to deliver) to purchasers and suppliers respectively. There is however an intermediate stage of disaggregation of the supply plans and its specification in terms of the assortment of inputs. This takes place via negotiations between the consuming and supplying enterprises through the appropriate Gossnab organ.

It is important to remember, as has already been indicated, that the Gossnab as well as the Gosplan may be involved in the planning of the allocation of resources. The following quotation outlines in greater detail the planning of supplies via Gossnab organs:

... enterprises and consumer organizations calculate their specific demand for materials on the basis of their production or construction programme and submit their specifications to the regional material and technical supply bodies. The latter summarise them for their own particular region, decide on the most rational forms of supply (direct or from warehouses) and submit the summary specifications to the All-Union central supply and sales organizations attached to the

Gossnab (i.e. the soyuzglavsnabsbyty AFF). On the basis
of this declared specific demand for output, and the
coordination of the product-range production plans with
the production ministries and government departments,
the All-Union central supply and sales organizations
link consumers with supplier and allocate orders for
the manufacture and delivery of output.   In the case
of output that is not allocated centrally (cement,
some building materials, chemicals etc.) the All-Union
central supply and sales organizations define the re-
gions of consumption for suppliers, which enables the
regional supply bodies to establish contact with particular consumers and issue orders for the delivery
of output to enterprises.
(Berry, Planning a Socialist Economy, pp.93-94)

Ultimately however the aggregation of requirements for specific goods will end up with the Gosplan. Should the aggregation
of these indents present the planners with imbalances then there
are five basic options available to them.   Firstly, increase
the planned output of the deficit commodity, secondly increase
imports, thirdly order a reduction on the inter-industry demand
for the deficit commodity, fourthly plan a reduction in the final
demand for that commodity and finally, run down inventories, if
available . As the Gosplan would be reticent to vary the vector of final demand given the inter-industry secondary effects
that this would produce, greater reliance is placed on the third
over the fourth method. This is particularly true if the goods
involved are not consumed directly but are themselves inputs in
the production of final goods. The third option is usually expressed in efforts to increase the efficiency of use by decreasing norms of utilisation.   This however is another indication
not so much of the problem of plan consistency as that of taut
planning - a point that will be raised repeatedly in the following chapters.
Following the 1965 reforms a renewed effort was made to
decentralise the unwieldy system of supply by establishing direct and long-term links between enterprises.   These links of
supply were first worked out by the relevant soyuzglavsnabsbyt
and the glavsnasbsbyt of the ministry concerned and then the
enterprises were left alone to settle the details and repeat
their orders over time. Table 2.3 sets out the number of goods
and enterprises involved in this direct linkage of supply system.   The source of this table does not give a detailed breakdown of the categories, types etc. of the goods involved.
Another source adds:

At present time (book published in 1973 AFF) more than
24% of rolled steel, approximately 30% of sodium car-
bonate, 60% of paper, 90% of wood pulp, 73% of synthetic
rubber etc. are being delivered according to the plan

Gossnab and the Industrial Supply System

of long-term links,
                    (Berry, Planning a Socialist Economy, p.96)

More recent information summarised in Table 2.4 indicates that
direct linking is of considerable importance in a number of
sectors.

TABLE 2.3   Direct links between enterprses

Year	Consumer enterprises	Supplier enterprises	No. of groups of goods
1966	1,403	543	383
1967	4,340	1,021	565
1968	5,867	1,564	826
1969	7,262	2,369	1,032
1970	10,206	2,804	1,276
1971	11,377	2,989	1,366
1972	11,760	3,210	1,260
1973	16,500	3,500	1,358
1974	20,000	5,000	1,500

Source: Kurotchenko Material'no-tekhnicheskoe ...
          p.112

TABLE 2.4   Goods subject to direct link supplies

Goods	Percentage of supply via direct links
Ferrous metals	42
Non-ferrous metals	51
Cement	82
Asbestos	93
Bearings	77
Motor car tyres	88
Sulphuric acid	60
Paper (newsprint and books)	73

Source: Ekonomicheskaya Gazeta No.41, Oct. 1979

The degree to which the development of direct links increases flexibility in the supply function of enterprises vis-a-
vis other enterprises is still very uncertain. There have been
no steps to allow contracting enterprises to set prices - a pre-
requisite in making suppliers more responsive to consumers'
needs. It is also important to remember that the direct links
system was set up and supervised by the Gossnab and still covers
a relatively small amount of commodity groups. In addition to
this there are some doubts as to the effectiveness of the legal
and financial penalties for breach of contract, if such a breach
allows the supplying enterprise to fulfil its own plan.   In
other words, there might be a positive trade-off in terms of,
say, bonuses for fulfilling output targets rather than the contracted assortment plan even if that means paying a fine for
late or non-delivery of supplies. The system of direct link-
ages will be maintained during the eleventh FYP but there are
signs that the authorities are somewhat disillusioned by the
relative lack of success. The problem appears to be loose discipline in delivering the contracted supplies. In a number of
occasions the appropriate ministry intervened and apparently
forbade the establishment of a direct contract(10).
The planners have experimented repeatedly with different
approaches to industrial supply. Dyker(11) summarised thus
some developments in the allocation of funded and non-funded
goods:

> ... Funding strictly means that the commodities in
> question are directly allocated by Gosplan to the
> ministries, while nonfunded commodities may be planned
> at any level of the planning and supply network. There
> were indeed only 277 funded commodities in 1971 ... In
> practice, however, the phrase bez fondov is often used
> in the sense of bez naryadov - without allocation cert-
> ificate as with the system that has been in operation
> in certain areas since 1966 in relation to the supply
> of certain oil products, construction materials and
> chemicals. A system of 'supply on the basis of orders'
> (snabzhenie po zakazam) in the construction section
> was experimentally introduced in six enterprises in
> 1970, and is presumably a development of nonallocational
> supply for the building industry. A decree passed in
> 1969 provided for the transfer of whole enterprises on
> to nonallocational supply in certain cases. Dispensing
> with the naryad clearly represents a significant degree
> of decentralisation and some moderation of the command
> principle. However there is no evidence that non-funded
> sales through the snabsbyt system involve any freedom
> of price formation. In addition, it is not clear to
> what extent enterprises may be permitted to 'shop
> around' among snabsbyt in different areas ...

Some further developments during the eleventh FYP include the signing of direct supply agreements between the Gossnab and its organs and enterprises. The idea is that the Gossnab itself rather than the supplying enterprises will guarantee deliveries of inputs. This however will involve an expansion of the size of inventories held by Gossnab and its organs. As will be shown in Section 2.2 below this may well be the beginning of transforming the Gossnab from a planner of supplies to a centralized inventories holder. This development would be indeed a radical departure from Gossnab's functions and a further step in the centralization of decision making in the planning system of the USSR. The implication of these developments and some further evidence are examined in greater detail in Chapter 3, Section 3.3 and Chapter 4, Section 4.5 of this book.

2.3 THE GOSSNAB AND THE ENTERPRISE AS SUPPLIERS

In analysing the behaviour of the Soviet industrial enterprise it is important to draw attention to a potential conflict within its objectives. The enterprise as a user of inputs has every interest to ensure an adequate and regular supply of the goods it uses. Hence it will try to apply for more inputs than absolutely necessary in order to ensure fulfilment of its own output plan. Similarly, the enterprise as a producer has an output plan to fulfil. Part or even all its output may well be the input of another enterprise. The conflict that can arise here is that in fulfilling its output plan, the enterprise may frustrate the attempt of the customer-enterprises in fulfilling theirs. For example it may deliver the wrong assortment or quality or delay deliveries of goods.
The Gossnab and its organs have their own plan to fulfil, i.e. to ensure the correct assortment, timing and delivery of supplies. Following the 1965 economic reforms that emphasised profitability and changed the incentives scheme, the Gossnab supply system was gradually integrated within the 'khozraschet' framework. In 1971 new rules came into operation concerning the planning and incentive schemes of supply organs(12). The basic planned targets and indexes were as follows:

(a) The supply of goods (expressed in natural units) to consuming enterprises as per the nomenclature of the Gosplan or Gossnab or of the relevant ministry and its departments.
(b) Total commodity flow (tovarooborot) including goods in transit and supplies out of inventories and stocks.
(c) The wages fund and related payments for management.
(d) Gross profit and profitability.
(e) Payments to receipts from the state budget.
(f) Capital expenditure.

There was also a system of bonuses based around the Material

Incentives Fund (MIF) which is formed from profits. Payments of bonuses was subject to plan fulfilment especially items (a), (b) and (d) above. By the mid-1970s only a very limited number of Gossnab organs were operating under the 1971 'khozraschet' system or had established incentive schemes according to the planned targets etc. outlined above. It appears however that the authorities are at present engaged in one more drive to strengthen the influence of 'khozraschet' in the supply side of planning during the eleventh FYP(13). Be that as it may, the Gossnab and its organs have still a basic task to execute, that of marrying suppliers and consumers. There are three basic problems in executing this plan given the characteristic behaviour of the subordinate enterprises. These are:

(a) To ensure that the planned quantities of goods are delivered on time and according to the assortment plan.
(b) To ensure that the production capacity of the enterprises is used fully and that input utilisation is kept at a minimum.
(c) To ensure that there is enough slack in the system in order to cover contingencies but at the same time minimise waste.

For the point of view of enterprises (b) may well conflict with (c), especially if the slack must not be revealed to the planners, thus leading to all the familiar problems regarding the execution of (a). The role and function of the Gossnab vis-a-vis the supply role of the enterprises and the objectives of the Gossnab itself can now be seen as part and parcel of the built-in tautness in Soviet plans.
Berliner summarised this point in the following manner:

> It has long been known that the weakness of the system of inter-enterprise supply has been a major shortcoming of Soviet economic organisation ... outside observers continue to report that "the most salient fact of economic life for the Soviet manager has been the inadequate provision of resources necessary to fulfil the enterprise plan". ... It would be an error however to attribute the problem of the Soviet supply system to the socialist basis of property ownership. A sufficient explanation may be found in the prevailing state of disequilibrium that characterises inter-enterprise transactions in the Soviet Union. The disequilibrium is due in part to economic policy, particularly to the policy of excessive taut planning.
> (The Innovation Decision, pp.61-62)

The conclusion is that attempting to examine the role of the Gossnab as a separate individual institution in the same way that, say, one would approach a capitalist firm or the Yugoslav

43

labour-managed enterprise is ultimately an unrewarding exercise as one will have to cross-refer continuously to enterprise behaviour in particular and to key characteristics of Soviet planning in general. In examining enterprise behaviour one is examining a part of the supply mechanism because enterprises reflect in their behaviour their own reactions to the aims of the Gossnab.

This particular conclusion is all the more realistic given that the Gossnab, so far, is a relatively insignificant direct supplier of inputs. For example Tables 2.5 and 2.6 indicate that with minor exceptions more than 70% of all inventories were held by enterprises rather than the supply organs.

TABLE 2.5   Yearly average distribution of production inventories and finished goods in industry and in the material technical supply system   (% of total)

Inventory types	1965	1970	1972
Production inventories	76.2	77.2	77.0
Finished goods	12.8	10.1	10.3
Goods within the material-technical supply system	11.0	12.7	12.7

Source: Kurotchenko, Material'no-tekhnicheskoe ... p.147. The data are for the whole USSR. The source does not specify the structure of inventories held by the supply system itself i.e. the percentage of finished goods and those to be used as inputs. See however Table 2.6.

An additional piece of evidence is the continuously growing Inventory/Output ratio in the Soviet industry from about 0.164 in the early 1970s, to 0.233 by 1980(14).   This may well be interpreted as an attempt by the industrial enterprises at greater self-sufficiency vis-a-vis inventory supplies. It may indicate greater reluctance to rely on other enterprises to supply the necessary input at all, or in time, or to rely on the capacity of the Gossnab to guarantee supplies. It can also, of course, be interpreted as another sign of the inefficient use of resources by Soviet industry, although this would not explain its cause.

The discussion so far has emphasised the supply function of the various institutions with respect to intermediate but not to final customers/consumers. Since consumers (in terms of

TABLE 2.6   End year distribution of inventories held (percentage of total inventories). Data for 1972. Figures in brackets are for 1965-66, where available.

Product	Producing enterprises	Gossnab depots etc.	Consuming enterprises
Rolled-ferrous metal	2.1 (3.3)	21.0 (8.2)	76.9 (88.5)
Finished ferrous metal	1.7 (3.0)	23.0 (9.5)	75.3 (87.5)
Tubing	3.3 (3.3)	36.3 (12.7)	60.4 (84.0)
Steel cables	4.6 (5.6)	15.3 (4.5)	80.1 (89.9)
Soda (calcium)	10.5 (6.1)	3.2 (2.3)	86.2 (91.6)
Soda (caustic)	4.8 (7.2)	9.2 (6.4)	86.0 (86.4)
Cement	35.7 (31.0)	-	64.3 (68.9)
Soft roofing materials	5.3 (5.9)	10.1 (6.1)	84.6 (88.0)
Diesel fuel	9.8 (10.1)	40.2 (29.2)	50.0 (60.2)
Mazut	6.0 (6.4)	8.1 (17.4)	85.9 (76.2)
Insulated electrical wires	5.9	8.1	86.0
Drawn wires	7.7	19.8	72.5
Lighting flex	9.8	24.8	65.4

Source: Kurotchenko, Material'no-tekhnicheskoe ... p.148
Some figures do not add up fully because of rounding.

the population at large) do not have a plan to fulfil neither do they receive naryady and zakazy, then it is not surprising that the literature has emphasised the behaviour of the enterprises and its supervisory organs as producer and consumer of inputs rather than producer of goods for final consumption by the people. In fact Soviet literature deals only peripherally, if at all, with the issue of the relations between enterprises and the Gossnab. Extending the present analysis to the production → supply → final consumption circuit would involve topics outside the mainstream of this book, namely the planning of consumption, incomes and prices. Hence in appraising enterprise behaviour, its supplying role will be seen primarily in terms of supplying inputs to other enterprises. This will raise however a number of important issues that require brief but careful consideration and justification.

Firstly, the problem of plan inconsistency will appear from the point of view of the enterprise as a consumer of inputs, as shortages in the goods necessary for it to fulfil its own plan. This may arise either because planners allocated too few inputs to allow the enterprise to produce its planned output or because the allocated inputs did not arrive at all, or if they did, they were of the wrong type or quality or were delayed. Plan inconsistency at this instance may be the outcome of taut planning i.e. of pressure exerted by planners on enterprises to ensure maximum effort and capacity utilization. The problem of tautness in planning and its relationship to the supply of inputs will be examined in detail in Chapter 4 of this book.

Secondly, the role of the enterprise as a supplier of final consumer goods to retail shops or directly to consumers needs separate consideration. It is tempting to assume that if the supplies in question are directed to consumers, then plan inconsistency may cease to be a problem, in the sense that consumers can be deemed to be residual users. In other words if the enterprise either does not deliver at all its planned output of consumer goods or delivers the wrong assortment, then the 'only' consequence of that will be consumer dissatisfaction. So the consequences here are differentiated from the chain effect on other enterprises, and therefore on the production of other goods, as in the case of nondelivery of production inputs.

There is of course massive documented and anecdotological evidence on the general insensitivity of Soviet planners towards consumers' preferences and of the lack of direct links between expressed consumers' preferences and the production plans of the enterprise. It is of course also true that enterprises are expected to fulfil their plans irrespective of whether these are for intermediate inputs or consumer goods. Indeed in both the tenth and the eleventh FYPs there is considerable and persistent emphasis on fulfilling the production plans of high quality goods and of consumer goods. Breaches of the assortment plan are penalised. All these particular points that pertain to the function of the enterprise as a supplier (irrespective of the type of goods) will be examined in detail in the appropriate Chapters and sections of this book. There is however one particular issue that will need clarification at this juncture, and this is, the popular and widespread belief that planners in general, and Soviet ones in particular, treat the consumer goods sector as a 'buffer'. In other words, when inconsistencies, shortages etc. appear in the overall balance of the economy, the vector of consumer demand is treated as variable and used to adjust the total output mix. It must be stressed that the issue here is a macroeconomic one and may not be of direct relevance to the operation of any single enterprise - which is what concerns us here. Keeping this point in mind, the evidence such as it is, contradicts the belief that the suppliers of consumer goods are the first to suffer when imbalances appear.

Portes and Winter(15) using data for Czechoslovakia, GDR Hungary and Poland spanning the mid-1950s to 1975, came to the following conclusions. Utilising an aggregate supply curve for consumption goods they found that with the possible exception of GDR, the planners did not use consumption goods as a buffer to absorb unfavourable events leading to output plan underfulfilment for the total output of the economy.   Specifically:

> ... [the results] ... indicate that in Czechoslovakia and Hungary planners tend to protect consumption when total output falls below trend ... For the GDR consumption is clearly protected in the short run.   In the long run this may not be true ... The results show both similarities in planners' responses in the four countries and differences in their choice of instruments. It may be possible to divide the group in two. The planners in Czechoslovakia and Hungary protect consumption from deviations in the final output and other competing end uses. Consumption-goods supply responds to deviations of agricultural output from its trends. In Poland and the GDR, consumption is adjusted as total output deviates from trend, on a roughly proportional basis ...
>
> (Portes and Winter, pp.362-3)

The position in the Soviet Union appears to have certain similarities with the four countries just examined, although the conclusions are far from certain.

Green and Higgins(16) developed a model which attempted to explore the extent by which aggregate consumption in the Soviet Union was a residual determined by overall supply or was dependent on other variables. Consumption was defined as expenditures on food, soft goods, durables and services.   Three alternative specifications (with one further variation added later on) were used:

(a) Expenditures on investment, defence, administration, inventory changes, net exports etc. were subtracted from gross national product providing an estimate of aggregate consumption. This was a polar case of supply determining aggregate consumption.

(b) The role of household consumption was introduced explicitly in the model by adding real household disposable income in supply-constrained consumption functions.

(c) A variation of (b) allowing explicitly for the shares of each categories of goods in consumption.

The results of the econometric investigation were as follows:

> Alternatives were compared as single equations.   By conventional criteria all provided similar adequate explanations of Soviet consumption patterns from the mid-1950s to 1972. When embedded in the economy-wide

> model, the scheme with explicit income effects on com-
> ponents was slightly superior in tracking the historical
> path of consumption ... Taking all system tests into
> account, the form in which aggregate consumption is
> partially determined by income performed as well as or
> better than the more completely supply-determined
> representations.   (Green and Higgins, pp.175-6)

Although the Soviet evidence is by no means conclusive, at least
it indicates that the extreme version of the textbook model of
planned economies where consumption is completely supply dom-
inated and acts as a residual is neither the best explanation
nor the only one available.

2.4 CONCLUSIONS

The role of 'supplier' in the Soviet framework can be examined
in two parts. Firstly, the enterprise itself as a supplier of
inputs, secondly, the Gossnab as a purveyor of both information
over supplies and input utilisation norms. Even if all Gossnab
departments were under 'khozraschet', the only way that the Gossnab could have been examined as a separate entity would have
been if it operated as a giant inventory-holder and wholesaler.
In the Soviet context, this is unreal, at least for the present
time, as shown by the statistical evidence on inventories and
'indirect' supplying via Gossnab depots. Treating the individual
organs of the Gossnab as separate enterprises (assuming always
that they do operate under 'khozraschet') would not add any exp-
lanatory value to the behaviour of the industrial enterprise.
The depots, wholesale stores etc. would have their own plans to
fulfil and hence would be subject to similar pressures of those
of the producer enterprises. The Gossnab organs in order to
ensure fulfilment of their own delivery-supply plans would
pressurise the enterprises under their jurisdiction to fulfil
on time their own output plans. But this is already a characteristic of Soviet planning. As Wiles observed: (17)

> If there were neither excess demand nor planner's ten-
> sion a command economy without raznaryadka could be
> quite normal; though ideology would undoubtedly stand
> in its way. The raznaryadka is technically justified
> only as a means of observance of priorities when there
> is tension.

(Raznaryadka is list of customers to which certain quantities
of products must be sent.)
     As the aims of the Gossnab come into conflict with that of
the enterprises it services, then its role has to be analysed
within the system of taut planning in the Soviet Union.   The
conflict between the Gossnab and the enterprises arise basically

in two areas, firstly input allocation vs planned output (taut planning) and the assortment plan vs total output. Given the pervasive influence of the Gossnab, it may well be useful at this stage to give a synopsis of the ways in which the Gossnab, its institutions and influence will make an appearance explicitly or implicitly in the following Chapters.

Firstly, in Chapter 3 it will be shown that the degree of the fulfilment of the assortment plan of a multiproduct enterprise will be crucially dependent on the detail of the input plan and the strictness by which the Gossnab is willing or able to enforce it. The planning and execution of the assortment plan will show yet again the Gossnab in its dual role as both a planner of inputs and output.

Secondly, Chapter 4 on tautness, contains an extensive section on the role and availability of unofficial (unplanned) inputs and the predictability of the behaviour of the enterprise when input plans change. This, taken in conjunction with the very important role of inventories and the relative insignificance of the Gossnab and its organs in this field, sets the discussion on tautness on a more general level. The Gossnab is treated as one of the pressure points on enterprises (input-wise) with the Gosplan being the other (output-wise).

Thirdly, in the discussion on the role of bonuses Gossnab appears less explicitly since success indicators are mostly output rather than input based. The influence of the Gossnab however is present all the time through the role of plan tautness (defined in the general way as expounded in Chapter 4) and the willingness or capacity of enterprises to earn bonuses.

Notes

1. I.D. Fasolyak and P.V. Smirnov, Organizatsiya i plan-irovanie snabzheniya i cbyta v narodnom khozyaistve, obyedinen-iyakh i na predpriyatiyakh, Moscow 1975, pp.30-113.

2. P.V. Smirnov, Organizatsiya i planirovanie sbyta promyshlennosti produktsii v SSSR, Moscow 1975, pp.23-57.

3. S. Sh. Zamaleev, Ekonomika otraslei narodnoyo khoz-yaistva, Kiev 1976, p.304.

4. L. Berry (Ed.), Planning a Socialist Economy Vol.2, Moscow 1977, p.95.

5. C.A. Krylov, The Soviet Economy, Lexington Books, Massachusetts 1979, pp.55-56.

6. M. Ellman, Soviet Planning Today, Cambridge University Press, Cambridge 1971, p.62. See also, M. Chistyakov, 'Metodicheskie ukazaniya k sostavleniya odinnadtsatogo pyatile-tnego plana', Voprosy Ekonomiki, No.1, 1981, p.113.

7. Chistyakov, Metodicheskie ukazaniya ..., p.113.

8. The basis of the supply plan itself can be found in H.S. Levine 'The Centralised Planning of Supply in Soviet Indu-stry' in Comparisons of the US and Soviet Economies, US Govern-ment Printing Office, Washington DC 1959, pp.151-176.

9. N.G. Chumachenko (Ed.), Metodologiya normirovaniya raskhoda material'nykh resursov v promyshlennom proizvodstve, Kiev 1976, p.63.

10. Ekomicheskaya Gazeta, No.41, Oct. 1979.

11. D. Dyker, 'Decentralization and the Command Principle - Some Lessons, from Soviet Experience', Journal of Comparative Economics, Vol.5, No.2, June 1981, p.133. See also Ekon. Gazeta, No.41, Oct. 1979.

12. The discussion in this section draws from V.S. Kurotchenko and A.I. Baskina (Eds.), Ekonomika Material'no - teknicheskogo snabzheniya, Moscow 1977, Chapter 3 passim, V.S. Kurotchenko and K. Gyurman, Ekonomicheskoe stimuliro-vanie v material'no-tekhnicheskom snabzhenii, Moscow 1977, passim, and Ekonomicheskaya Gazeta, No.34, August 1978.

13. Ekonomicheskaya Gazeta No.41, October 1979.

14. Calculated from data in Narodnoe Khozyaistvo for var-ious years as the ratio of material inventories held by enter-prises/Gross value of industrial output at wholesale prices. See also G. Schroeder, 'The Reform of the Supply System in the Soviet Industry', Soviet Studies, Vol.24, No.3, July 1972, pp. 97-119.

15. R. Portes and D. Winter, 'The Supply of Consumption Goods in Centrally Planned Economies', Journal of Comparative Economics, Vol.1, No.4, Dec. 1977, pp.351-65.

16. D.W. Green and C.I. Higgins, Sovmod I: A Macroecon-omic Model of the Soviet Union, Academic Press, New York 1977, Ch.6.

17. P.J.D. Wiles, The Political Economy of Communism, Basil Blackwell, Oxford 1964, p.182.

CHAPTER THREE

MODELS OF THE SOVIET INDUSTRIAL ENTERPRISE

3.1 INTRODUCTION

This chapter contains three sections. The first outlines briefly
some early models of the Soviet enterprise developed by western
authors.   Most of these models are very simple, some of them
even unrealistic compared to actual Soviet theory and practice.
They serve a purpose however, in highlighting some aspects of
Soviet enterprise behaviour, including a crude supply function,
and thus set the scene for the second section which contains
two models.   The first is a multi-product, multi-input model
designed to illustrate some of the assortment plan problems
facing Soviet planners and also to introduce certain points
concerning input utilisation and the Gossnab supply plan.   The
second model is a simpler one involving one good only and is
designed to illustrate through a series of comparative static
exercises the problem of planned target compatibility in the
Soviet enterprise model.   Unlike the first model that discusses
the input plan and certain aspects of input plan tautness, the
second does not.   Plan tautness is discussed in greater detail
in Chapter 4.

A particular point that will arise in all the models
presented here concerns the exact definition of the input
plan which acts as a constraint on the level of output (either
total or the assortment) that can be achieved by the enterprise.
In terms of the institutional framework under which Soviet
enterprises operate, this will be taken to mean the inputs
allocated by the Gossnab, its organs and by the supervising
bodies of the enterprise.   Even if some of these inputs are
decentrally allocated, they will still be allocated by a
superior organ rather than purchased freely by the enterprise
itself.   The input constraints will be further reinforced
by the overall flow of funds plan within which the enterprise operates and which is supervised by the Gosbank (control
by the ruble).   Although enterprises enjoy a greater freedom
in matching income with expenditure, say, through leads or
lags in payments and receipts, this is not matched by a

similar freedom in obtaining inputs for which there are no allocation certificates. The only case where the enterprise does
have some freedom of input choice is in that of labour. Within
the planned wages fund, the composition of the labour force may
well vary (unskilled/skilled/blue collar etc.), and as there is
no centralised system of labour allocation the enterprises do
rely on a relatively free labour market for their labour inputs.
In fact, some 90% of all new hiring is done at the 'factory gates'
i.e. through direct negotiation between the workers and the management.(1) The wage rates payable however are set out by the
authorities, and even allowing any conscious effort on the part
of the management to entice labour by lax enforcement of skill
grading and therefore the payment of higher wage rates, the total
spent on labour is limited by the planned size of the wages fund.
Some aspects of this potential flexibility in use of inputs
within the input plan is discussed in the following section.

3.2 SIMPLE MODELS OF THE ENTERPRISE

A common characteristic of the modelling of any production
units is the specification of an objective function which is
then maximised or minimised either freely or subject to some
constraint. This particular approach developed within the neoclassical model of the firm was apparently well-suited for application to the Soviet enterprise.
     The production unit (either the enterprise or the associ-
ation) receives a plan: usually a set of minimum levels of
performance and the maximum amount of inputs that can be used
to achieve them. The incentive of the production unit to stick
by and carry out the plan is expressed in terms of bonuses that
reward fulfilment and penalise deviations from the plan.   The
relevant system, however, must be somehow specified within the
preferences of the 'congeries of people' that constitute the
decision-makers of the enterprise. Hence the necessity to introduce some kind of managerial utility function that will allow these preferences to be expressed within the constraints of
the plan and the desire to earn bonuses.
     Most of the earliest models of the Soviet enterprise that
were developed by western authors stuck fairly closely to the
following pattern: an objective function which contained the
level of output or profits or profitability was maximised subject to an inputs constraint. The objective function was either
a general one, usually containing output as its main argument,
or was defined in terms of a managerial utility function which
normally contained indirectly the bonuses to be earned by carrying out the plan. A typical example of these earlier approaches can be drawn from the work of Ward(2).
     This model specifies a very general bonus function in the
form of

Models of the Soviet Industrial Enterprise

$$G = G(\pi, Q, x_1 \ldots x_n) \tag{3.1}$$

where

$$\pi = \sum_{i=1}^{n} P_i x_i \text{ is profit}$$

with

$x_i \ldots x_k$ being output and $P_1 \ldots P_k$ being fixed output prices

$x_{k+1} \ldots x_n$ being inputs i.e. negative outputs in the sense that they are consumed rather than produced by the enterprise with

$P_{k+1} \ldots P_n$ being their fixed prices.

$$Q = \sum_{i=1}^{k} P_i x_i \text{ is the global value of output.}$$

The bonus function is general enough to encompass various possibilities. For example bonuses are derived from increasing profits, increasing global output, increasing the output of specific goods or decreasing the use of specific inputs, such as savings on energy etc. In such a simple and generalised model the role of input or output plans does not appear at all. Indeed Ward specifically states that the model is applicable to enterprises which may or may not fulfil their norms.

The bonus function (3.1) is then maximised subject to a transformation function with λ being the Lagrangean multiplier.

$$F(x_1 \ldots x_n) = 0 \tag{3.2}$$

The expressions G_π, G_Q, G_{x_i} refer to the marginal contributions of the three arguments to the bonuses received by manager. Their actual numerical value would be ascertainable by specifying exactly the bonus function. The first order conditions are:

$$\frac{\partial G}{\partial x_i} = G_\pi P_i + G_Q P_i + G_{x_i} - \lambda F_{x_i} = 0 \qquad \text{for } i = 1 \ldots k \text{ output} \tag{3.3}$$

$$\frac{\partial G}{\partial x_i} = G_\pi P_i + G_{x_i} - \lambda F_{x_i} = 0 \quad \text{for } i = k+1 \ldots n \text{ inputs} \tag{3.4}$$

Rearranging (3.3) gives

$$\frac{1}{\lambda} = \frac{F_{x_i}}{P_i(G_\pi + G_Q) + G_{x_i}} \qquad \text{for } i = 1 \ldots k \text{ output} \tag{3.5}$$

where $1/\lambda$ can be interpreted in terms of the shadow price of the material or moral incentives of producing the maximum output possible under constraint (3.2). It would also follow that for any two outputs, say x_1 and x_2, the rate of transformation in production would be

$$\frac{F_{x_1}}{F_{x_2}} = \frac{P_1(G_\pi + G_Q) + G_{x_1}}{P_2(G_\pi + G_Q) + G_{x_2}} \tag{3.6}$$

The rate of transformation depends on the relative output prices and the contributions of the two goods to bonuses. Conflicts may now arise in the fulfilment of the assortment plan (which of course is not included in Ward's simple model) if the relative prices and the bonus element made it profitable for the enterprise to shift resources, and therefore the product mix, in the opposite direction to that indicated by the plan.

An alternative approach used by Balassa involved the introduction of an explicit bonus function as the maximand(3). Managers of the enterprise are assumed to be bonus maximisers on the basis that they received a percentage of the realised profits and a percentage of the value of output produced over that of the planned level. The maximand was expressed as

$$B = m(PQ - Lw - K) + n(PQ - T) \tag{3.7}$$

where P is the fixed price of output Q, L and w are labour and fixed wage rate, K is the value of the fixed amount of capital available - labour being the only variable input, and T being the planned value of output. The coefficients $0 < m, n < 1$ determine the percentage of profits and above-plan output that will be paid into the bonus fund.

Maximizing with respect (3.7) to L gives

$$\frac{\partial B}{\partial L} = m\left[p\frac{\partial Q}{\partial L} - w\right] + np\frac{\partial Q}{\partial L} = 0 \quad \text{and rearranging to}$$

$$p\frac{\partial Q}{\partial L} = \left(\frac{m}{m+n}\right)w \tag{3.8}$$

Since profit maximisation requires $p\frac{\partial Q}{\partial L} = w$ and output maximisation $p\frac{\partial Q}{\partial L} = 0$ then it follows that as long as $(m/m+n) < 1$ and $m > 0$, the level of output would be somewhere between that of a profits and an output maximiser. By varying the size of m and n planners could affect the level of output that would maximise bonus.

A simple rearrangement of equation (3.8) gives

$$m\left(p\frac{\partial Q}{\partial L} - w\right) = -n\left(p\frac{\partial Q}{\partial L}\right) \tag{3.9}$$

i.e. m (marginal profit from labour) = -n (marginal revenue from labour). It then follows that bonus is maximised when an additional amount of labour employed does not add anything to the bonus because it either decreases (increases) revenue or increases (decreases) profitability.

Models of the Soviet Industrial Enterprise

Although Balassa's model concerns a single product enterprise, equation (3.9) can be extended to cover a multi-product one:

$$P_i \frac{\partial Q_i}{\partial L_i} = \left(\frac{m}{m+n}\right) w \qquad i = 1 \ldots n \text{ goods} \qquad (3.9a)$$

with L_i and P_i being the amount of labour used in the production of the ith output, P_i being the product price. An enterprise will attempt to allocate the labour amongst the production of different goods in order to equalise the marginal revenue product of labour in the production of that good, [LHS of (3.9a)] to the weighted wage cost. In real life, of course, the enterprise would be given an assortment and an input plan, but not in enough detail so as to deprive the enterprise manager of all initiative over the actual use of inputs and their allocation over different goods. From equation (3.8) it would also follow that

$$P = MC \left(\frac{m}{m+n}\right), \text{ from Marginal Cost} = MC = w / \frac{\partial Q}{\partial L} \qquad (3.10)$$

Since different enterprises will have different production functions their MCs will be different. Fixing both P and m/m+n ensures that a given level of output within an industry is produced as cheaply as possible by equalising the MCs of all the enterprises. There is a problem here however in that the price so fixed may not cover the Average Cost of some enterprises and thus will lead to losses. This may well explain the reason why Soviet Ministries are allowed some discretion in setting the m and n coefficients for associations or enterprises under their jurisdiction(4). Alternatively, prices may be kept constant and by varying the individual m/m+n ratio for each enterprise output can be allocated towards enterprises with the lowest Marginal Cost. This however requires a very detailed amount of information concerning the production function of individual enterprises, not to mention the problems involved in justifying different bonus coefficients amongst enterprises producing similar goods or belonging to the same association.

Ames(5) extended and developed along similar lines a model of the Soviet enterprise by specifying a managerial utility function as

$$U = \alpha Q + (1 - \alpha)\pi \qquad (3.11)$$

where Q is output, π are profits defined as $PQ - C(Q)$, α a fixed coefficient and U 'a reward'. As Ames specifies that this is a utility and not a bonus function, then U is not rubles but the utility derived via producing Q and/or earning π. As the actual bonus function that produces the monetary rewards is not specified, it follows that α and $1 - \alpha$ are the marginal contributions to utility of producing one extra unit of output and earning one extra kopek or ruble of profits. The numerical value of α must be $0 < \alpha < 1$ because a value of $\alpha = 1$ would signify that

55

profits do not contribute to the managerial utility and therefore to bonuses. Maximising utility with respect to output Q and rearranging gives:

$$C'(Q) = MC = \frac{\alpha}{1-\alpha} + P \quad \text{or} \tag{3.12}$$

$$MC - P = \frac{\alpha}{1-\alpha}$$

Since $(\alpha/1-\alpha) > 0$, given $0 < \alpha < 1$, and as MC and P are expressed in money terms expression (3.12) can be interpreted as follows. The utility maximising manager will increase output past the level of profit maximisation (MC = P), the extent of the increase depending on the size of α. In other words as long as the difference between MC and the fixed price P was smaller than $\alpha/1-\alpha$ then it would pay to increase output. There are two problems here however. Firstly, the model will produce meaningful results only if MC is rising. Secondly, there is a problem with the numerical definitions. If P and MC are expressed in rubles then $\alpha/1-\alpha$ is kopeks. If however $0.5 < \alpha < 1$ and MC and P are expressed in kopeks, then their difference, a fraction of a

FIGURE 3.1 The output decision (Ames' model)

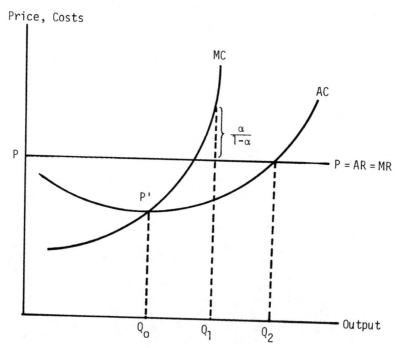

kopek, would be insignificant and the model would collapse back to a profits maximising situation since the marginal cost will be approximately equal to price.   The model is thus restricted in its uses and requires special assumptions both about the size of α and the definition of MC and P.

Taking now the case of increasing MCs, the less important profits are in the utility function of the manager of the enterprise the greater output will be.   In terms of Figure 3.1, if α increases (i.e. the weight of the output in the utility function) then output will increase from Q_1 but no more than Q_2 unless the enterprise is making planned losses.   Should the enterprise have been a pure output maximiser (with profits playing no role) then the average cost curve would serve as the supply function, as price of the good was varied by the planners.   For prices less than $P'Q_0$ the enterprise would have to be subsidised - i.e. make planned losses.   In the cases however, where the maximand is a weighted average of both profit and output, then a supply function can be derived as a curve relating different levels of output at different prices.   Output will increase up to a point where the difference between P and MC is equal to $\alpha/1 - \alpha$.   Given α, then the supply is purely a function of prices.   (See Figure 3.2.)

FIGURE 3.2   Supply curve (Ames' model)

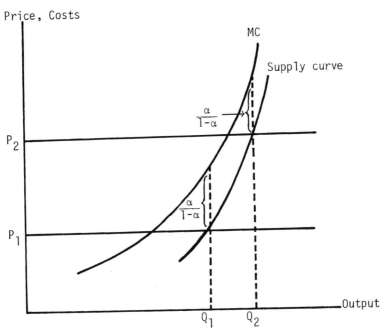

Price, Costs

MC

Supply curve

$\dfrac{\alpha}{1-\alpha}$

P_2

$\dfrac{\alpha}{1-\alpha}$

P_1

Output

Q_1 Q_2

Ames' exercise is interesting but hopelessly unreal because the model does not contain any input constraint and it overlooks the fact that wholesale industrial prices in the USSR are highly inflexible. In the context of this single product model, the assumption of price variation used to influence output is, of course, unreal. Prices however can be varied in order to influence product mix expecially if new or higher quality goods are involved(6). Ames also proceeded to derive a series of input demand functions, but comparative static results could not be signed unless production functions were explicitly defined.

A further variation on these simple models is to introduce profitability as the maximand subject to a sales plan. Defining the maximand as

$$R = \frac{PQ - \sum_{j=1}^{n} P_i x_i}{P^* x_j} = \frac{\pi}{P^* x_j} \qquad (3.13)$$

Subject to $PQ - S^* \geqslant 0$, where $\qquad\qquad (3.14)$

S^* is the minimum level of sales, R is the profit rate on capital employed, P^* is the cost price used to evaluate the amount of capital employed, P_1 is the cost of using capital (interest, rental payments etc.), x_1 is capital and P_j, x_j the prices and amount of the rest of inputs used. The level of output Q is a function of inputs $f(x_1 \ldots x_n)$ with sales PQ equalling the value of output produced, P being the fixed output price.

Maximizing (3.13) subject to (3.14) with respect to x_1 with λ being the Lagrangean multiplier, with the sales constraint binding:

$$P \frac{\partial Q}{\partial x_1} = P_1 + \left[\frac{P_1}{(1 + \lambda P^* x_1)} \left(\frac{\pi}{x_1 P_1} - \lambda P^* x_1 \right) \right] \qquad (3.15)$$

The level of capital utilisation will depend on the minimum sales plan but in general it can be shown to be less than that of a profit maximising enterprise. For example if the sales plan was not binding, then $\lambda = 0$ and the expression in the brackets in the RHS of (3.15) would be positive if $\pi > 0$. It would then follow that the enterprise would use capital up to the point where its marginal revenue product (MRP) equalled the price P_1 plus the expression in the brackets. The amount of capital employed would then be smaller than that used by a profit maximizer where the use would stop at MRP = P_1.

Despite the fact that this example does not include the influence of the input plan, it does illustrate an aspect of the discussion on the profit mark-up on cost. In section 1.5 of Chapter 1 it was indicated that in practice there is a built-in disincentive for the Soviet enterprise to use more capital unless the average costs of production (including interest payments where applicable) are likely to fall. Within the confines of this example it now also follows that the rate of substitution between inputs will be affected not only by their relative prices but also by the price of output. The constrained maximising conditions for x_j, $j = 2 \ldots n$, x_1 being capital, are:

$$P \frac{\partial Q}{\partial x_j} = P_j - \left[\frac{P_j \lambda P^* x_1}{1 + \lambda P^* x_1} \right]$$

with the sales constraint binding

$j = 2 \ldots n$ 　　　　(3.16)

and therefore

$$\frac{\partial x_1}{\partial x_j} \bigg]_{Q = \text{constant}} = \frac{P_j - B}{P_1 + A} \qquad j = 2 \ldots n \qquad (3.17)$$

where A and B are the bracketed expressions in equations (3.15) and (3.16) respectively. Both these expressions contain P the price of output.

This very simplified result hints at some problems that will be explored later. They concern the difficulties in reconciling the desire of the enterprise to stick to its objective - here maximise profitability - and the desire of the planners (esp. of the Gossnab) to maintain a fairly strict proportionality between inputs used and the level of output and at the same time to avoid output and input price changes. Proportional relationships between inputs and output are inherent in planning techniques that make use of input-output, material balances and norms, and of course, simplify the estimation task of the supply plan.

The profitability criterion besides affecting the desired input ratios as viewed from the enterprises' point of view may also affect the overall cost of production in a particular industry. For example minimising the average cost of production can be achieved by varying the profitability criterion, i.e. requiring the enterprises either to maximise the ratio of profits to total revenue or to total production costs. In Figure 3.3 assuming a constant price P, an enterprise maximising profits/total production costs must maximize AB/BQ_1. This is achieved by producing Q_1, where the AC is at minimum. Similarly maximisation of the profits/revenue requires maximising AB/AQ_1 then again leading to output Q_1. In either case the level of output is smaller than that of a profits maximising enterprise, Q_2. The level of output of an enterprise maximising profits/capital ratio will be smaller than Q_2, but without specific information on costs it cannot be determined a priori whether it would be bigger than Q_1. It is important to note however that if the enterprises have different cost structures, AC minimisation is not necessarily beneficial from the industry's point of view since some of them will have higher AC than others(7).

The profitability criterion in the bonus function however may affect the centralised investment decisions in undesirable ways(8). Assume a managerial objective function containing two

FIGURE 3.3   Cost minimisation and enterprise objectives

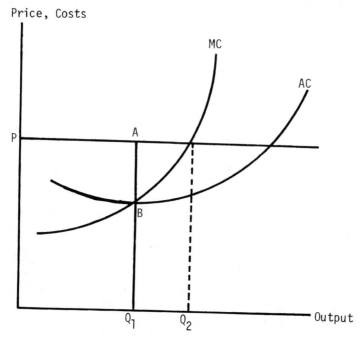

alternative forms of bonus schemes

$$A\left[\frac{\Pi}{K}\right] + B\left[\frac{Q - \bar{Q}}{\bar{Q}}\right] \qquad \text{or} \qquad (3.18)$$

$$C\left[\frac{\Pi}{K}\right] + D\left[\frac{\Pi - \bar{\Pi}}{\bar{\Pi}}\right] \qquad (3.19)$$

Π/K being a simple measure of profitability, and $\bar{Q}$, $\bar{\Pi}$ being the previous levels of output and profit. A, B, C and D are fixed coefficients. Managers are expected to maximise bonuses which in turn depend on profitability or the growth rate of profitability or output. Define a simple profits function as $PQ(K,L)$ - wL - rK with K and L being labour and capital used with r and w their respective prices (r here would be equal to P_1 in the previous multi-input example).

$$\Pi = P\,Q\,(K,\ L) - wL - rK \qquad (3.20)$$

The rates of factor substitution derived from (3.18) are

$$\frac{Q_L}{Q_K} = \frac{w}{r + \frac{\Pi}{K}} \qquad (3.21)$$

and from (3.19)

60

$$\frac{Q_L}{Q_K} = \frac{w}{r + (1 - \frac{1}{m})\frac{\Pi}{K}} \qquad \text{with } m = 1 + \frac{D\bar{\Pi}}{CK} \qquad (3.22)$$

From (3.21) it follows that $w/r > Q_L/Q_K$, so that the input combinations preferred by the enterprise will be less capital intensive compared to a cost minimising enterprise. This again reflects the results in equation (3.15) above. For expression (3.22) cost minimising conditions are achieved when $m = 1$. This occurs either when $D = 0$ so that the percentage increase in profits does not influence bonus, or when $C \to \infty$. In the latter case as long as profitability is non-zero the bonus will tend to infinity. Finally, but less plausibly, cost minimisation may also arise if $\bar{\Pi} = 0$.

The bonus scheme described by equations (3.18) and (3.19) may lead to rather perverse effects on the capital/labour ratio that enterprises would prefer to use if they were given the choice by Gossnab. The denominator of both equations (3.21) and (3.22) contains π/K. Given w/r and D and C, as profitability π/K decreased the relative price of labour would increase thus making less labour intensive (i.e. more capital intensive) processes desirable. So for two enterprises with different π/Ks the one with the higher π/K would favour more labour intensive processes, whereas the one with the lower would favour capital intensive techniques. This may lead to enterprises with relatively low profits per unit of capital employed pressing for, and attracting more, capital for their own use than enterprises with relatively higher capital profitability. It would also follow, however, that by varying the bonus function coefficients or giving enterprises in different sectors different bonus functions the demand for inputs can be manipulated from low to high profitability sectors.

The models outlined so far make a limited range of predictions concerning either the level of output or input utilisation(9). The one element of optimal resource utilisation that did enter the discussion was via the role of profitability and capital intensity of production. Given the low capital productivity in the Soviet Union in the 1960s through to the 1980s it is not surprising that the 1965 and 1972 economic reforms brought into prominence the role of profits and profitability. But as Zauberman(10) observed in appraising the various 'rules of the game' suggested for the Soviet enterprises since 1965, the question of rational use of resources and enterprise behaviour is, in the final analysis, inseparable from the question of pricing and investment decisions. Given the inflexibility of the industrial prices and the almost totally centralised control of investment funds, the best that planners can expect from the success indicators that they hand down to the enterprises is a flow of information. In other words parametric control of enterprises via changes in success indicators or bonus schemes is by definition the same as decentralisation of decision-making. As the first chapter of this book has indicated the formation of industrial associations and the relative insignificance of decentralised investment point consistently to a growing rather than a lessening degree of central control of enterprises.

3.3 AN EXERCISE IN MODEL BUILDING AND COMPARATIVE STATICS

Utilising the standard neoclassical tools of analysis of the theory of the firm and applying them to the Soviet enterprise can be both a complex and occasionally unrewarding exercise. In this section two fairly detailed models are built up; firstly a multi-product model incorporating some of the standard constraints imposed on the enterprise and secondly a single product model which is used as a vehicle for comparative statics analysis. It is important to state at the outset that no single model, however complex, can do justice or explain the behaviour of the Soviet enterprise. The reason for this will emerge as the analysis is developed. The reason for some differences in the specification of the two models (other than the obvious one of single vs multi product enterprise) is that it allows the exploration of different aspects of enterprise behaviour without making the model either so general that it explains nothing, or is so unreal as to make it a purely academic exercise.

The Multiproduct Model

As already indicated in Chapter 1 the enterprise is expected to fulfil several targets the most important of which still remains the level of sales. Thus the main maximand of the model will be the output of different goods weighted by their fixed prices. In a one-period model such as the one being developed here, fluctuations in the level of inventories of finished goods can be disregarded. In other words sales will equal value of output produced. This is not too unrealistic an assumption to make given the sellers' market in which enterprises operate. This assumption is further modified by the existence of an assortment as well as a sales plan that the multiproduct enterprise has to fulfil. In other words the enterprise will not only have to just produce and deliver its output, but it will also have to be of the right assortment. Customer enterprises have the right to reject, i.e. not purchase or accept delivery, of incorrect assortment. Indeed all the incentive schemes in the Soviet Union in the 1970s and 1980s include rules to the effect that:

(a) The value of goods whose assortment plan has not been fulfilled is deducted from the value of output.
(b) There can be no payments of bonuses for overfulfilling the output plan unless the assortment plan is fulfilled as well.

Given the seller's market in the Soviet Union the fixed output prices may appear of little relevance but it will be shown that they may affect assortment decisions as they enter into the determination of the size of profits.   The constraints on the maximand are therefore the assortment plan, the input plan and a minimum level of profits.

The sales target, assortment plans and profits are expressed in absolute terms although of course in the Soviet plan they are expressed in growth terms, i.e. x% increase over the base years. As the model developed here is strictly static - a one period analysis - this compromise does not affect the result. Two further points need to be raised.   Firstly there is no explicitly managerial utility function. By maximising sales the Soviet manager is expected to maximise the size of bonuses that depend on the fulfilment of the sales and assortment plan. Secondly, and most importment, the problem of plan tautness does not appear explicitly in this model.   This is for two reasons:

(a) In the case of the multiproduct enterprise input utilisation amongst different goods can give a rather unusual illustration of an aspect of plan tautness of inputs vis-a-vis outputs. So although in formal terms the enterprise does not (and cannot) breach its inputs constraint, tautness is explored indirectly.

(b) Plan tautness is examined in detail in Chapter 4 where a model of a single-product, sales maximising enterprise allows explicitly for input use outside the input allocation as set by the Gossnab. In addition to this the subsequent chapters on bonus schemes are essentially exercises on plan tautness and its effect on enterprise behaviour and plan fulfilment.

The multi-product enterprise can now be developed along the following lines.   The maximand is total sales

$$P_1^* \, Q_1 + P_2^* \, Q_2 \ldots P_n^* \, Q_n = \sum_{i=1}^{n} P_i^* \, Q_i \qquad (3.23)$$

with P_i^* and Q_i being the fixed prices and levels of output of goods $i = 1 \ldots n$. The production functions of the n individual goods are strictly concave with respect to inputs x_{ji}

$$Q_i = Q_i(x_{1i}, \, x_{2i}, \, \ldots \, x_{mi}), \quad i = 1 \ldots n \qquad (3.24)$$

where x_{ji} is the jth input (j = 1 ... m) used in the production of the ith good (i = 1 ... n)(11).

The enterprise operates subject to the following constraints

(a) An input plan for the m inputs used by the enterprise as set out by the allocation plan agreed by the Gossnab and its organs, or where appropriate, by the Ministries. As most of the inputs allocated in the input plan are expressed in physical terms this constraint is set out   in physical form. Enterprises, however, are expected to earn a minimum amount of profits so that input prices do enter into the decision-making. Input prices appear therefore in the profits constraint. The input constraint is written as

$$\bar{X}_j \geqslant \sum_{i=1}^{n} x_{ji} \qquad j = 1 \ldots m \text{ constraints} \qquad (3.25)$$

where $\bar{X}_1 \ldots \bar{X}_m$ is the total amount of inputs $1 \ldots m$ allocated for use in the production of $1 \ldots n$ goods. Given the fixed prices per unit of inputs $x_1 \ldots x_m$ as $P_1 \ldots P_m$ then the cost of producing good i is

$$\sum_{j=1}^{m} P_j \, x_{ji}$$

and the total cost of production of goods $Q_1 \ldots Q_n$ is

$$\sum_{i=1}^{n} \sum_{j=1}^{m} P_j \, x_{ji} \qquad (3.26)$$

(b) An assortment plan for each individual good produced. The plan is expressed here in value terms in order to allow for the influence of the relative prices of good on the choices, if any, made by the enterprise.

$$P_i^* Q_i (x_{1i} \cdots x_{mi}) \geqslant \bar{Q}_i \qquad i = 1 \ldots n \text{ constraints} \qquad (3.27)$$

where $\bar{Q}_1 \ldots \bar{Q}_n$ are the minimum planned level of output of goods $1 \ldots n$ in value terms. Given the infrequency of price changes in the Soviet Union it is quite realistic to assume that $\bar{Q}_1 \ldots \bar{Q}_n$ may change without any changes in $P_1^* \ldots P_n^*$. Prices of new or improved goods however are subject to negotiation or change. This however is not a relevant consideration in this static, one period model.

(c) A minimum profits plan:

$$\sum_{i=1}^{n} P_i^* Q_i - \sum_{i=1}^{n} \sum_{j=1}^{m} P_j \, x_{ji} \geqslant \bar{\Pi} \qquad (3.28)$$

with $\bar{\Pi}$ being the planned level of minimum profits. The actual practice is to set a minimum level of profitability expressed as a percentage of the capital employed. Introducing the profitability constraint as this point increases the complexity of the model without adding anything to its predictive value. Profitability and interest rate charges are all included explicitly in single product model developed in this section.

Forming now the Lagrangean system [max M]:

$$\left.\begin{array}{l} M = \sum_{i=1}^{n} P_i^* Q_i + \lambda_1 \left[P_1^* Q_1\ (\ ) - \bar{Q}_1 \right] + \ldots \\[2ex] \ldots + \lambda_n \left[P_n^* Q_n\ (\ ) - \bar{Q}_n \right] + \mu_1 \left[\bar{X}_1 - \sum_{i=1}^{n} X_{1i} \right] + \ldots \\[2ex] \ldots \mu_m \left[\bar{X}_m - \sum_{i=1}^{n} X_{mi} \right] + \phi \left[\sum_{i=1}^{n} P_i^* Q_i - \sum_{i=1}^{n} \sum_{j=1}^{m} P_j X_{ji} - \bar{\Pi} \right] \end{array}\right\} \quad (3.29)$$

with λ, μ, and ϕ being the Lagrangean multipliers.

Maximising with respect to x_{ji} and using the Kuhn-Tucker conditions:

$$\left.\begin{array}{l} \dfrac{\partial M}{\partial x_{11}} = P_1^* \dfrac{\partial Q_1}{\partial x_{11}} + \lambda_1 P_1^* \dfrac{\partial Q_1}{\partial x_{11}} - \mu_1 + \phi\ P_1^* \dfrac{\partial Q_1}{\partial x_{11}} - \phi P_1 \leqslant 0 \\[1ex] \quad\vdots \\[1ex] \dfrac{\partial M}{\partial x_{m1}} = P_1^* \dfrac{\partial Q_1}{\partial x_{m1}} + \lambda_1 P_1^* \dfrac{\partial Q_1}{\partial x_{m1}} - \mu_m + \phi P_1^* \dfrac{\partial Q_1}{\partial x_{m1}} - \phi P_m \leqslant 0 \\[1ex] \quad\vdots \\[1ex] \dfrac{\partial M}{\partial x_{mn}} = P_n^* \dfrac{\partial Q_n}{\partial x_{mn}} + \lambda_n P_n^* \dfrac{\partial Q_n}{\partial x_{mn}} - \mu_m + \phi P_n^* \dfrac{\partial Q_n}{\partial x_{mn}} - \phi P_m \leqslant 0 \end{array}\right\} \quad (3.30)$$

(The rest of the conditions for a maximum are omitted for the sake of simplicity.)

There are $m \times n$ equation above, i.e. n equation for each of the 1 ... n goods and m equations for each of the inputs. There are altogether $n + m + 1$ constraints (i.e. the assortment, inputs and profits constraints) but only n goods. As will be shown later on in the comparative statics exercise some of these constraints will be redundant. At this stage however this does not affect the results obtained.

In order to explore the economic implications of these conditions whilst at the same time simplifying the notation, it will be assumed that the constraints on the first two inputs and outputs are binding so that λ_1, λ_2, μ_1, μ_2 and therefore x_{11} x_{12} x_{21} x_{22} are all positive. The profit constraints is also assumed to be binding so that $\phi > 0$. These conditions could of course be generalised for any pair of inputs or outputs as long as the solutions are not interior. The equations relating to the use of input 1 in the output of goods 1 and 2 are

$$P_1^* \frac{\partial Q_1}{\partial Q_{11}} (1 + \lambda_1 + \phi) = \mu_1 + \phi P_1 \qquad (3.31)$$

$$P_2^* \frac{\partial Q_2}{\partial x_{12}} (1 + \lambda_2 + \phi) = \mu_1 + \phi P_1$$

and therefore

$$P_1^\star \frac{\partial Q_1}{\partial x_{11}} (1 + \lambda_1 + \phi) = P_2^\star \frac{\partial Q_2}{\partial x_{12}} (1 + \lambda_2 + \phi) \qquad (3.32)$$

It now follows that the enterprise will use input 1 in the production of goods 1 and 2 up to the point where its weighted marginal revenue product (MRP) is equal between the two goods. If the equality does not hold, the enterprise can increase the overall value of its output by switching inputs between goods. The price of the input does not matter as it will make the same contribution to costs. This assumption is relaxed further on when input transference costs are explicitly allowed for in this model. The shadow prices λ_1, λ_2 and ϕ indicate the value to the enterprise of variations in the assortment and profits plan in terms of the effects on its maximand, here the total value of output.

If there was no assortment plan or it was not binding ($\lambda_1 = \lambda_2 = 0$) then the only determinant of input use between the two goods would have been their relative prices. From equation (3.32) above

$$\frac{\partial Q_1}{\partial x_{11}} \bigg/ \frac{\partial Q_2}{\partial x_{12}} = \frac{P_2^\star}{P_1^\star} \qquad (3.33)$$

The lower the shadow price of fulfilling the assortment plan then the greater the influence of the relative price of goods in determining input use and therefore the level of output of the goods in question. The role of relative prices and the assortment plan has already been touched on in section 3.2 but in a simpler context. There is, however, an important difference here. The equilibrium conditions as depicted in equation (3.32) assume that the enterprise is completely free to transfer inputs from good to good in pursuing the objective of equalising the weighted MRPs. If the enterprise however was subject to very strict input allocation plan that specified which input would be used for what good, then it would follow that the relative prices of goods would be irrelevant in influencing input use and therefore the level of output of different goods. Enterprises subject to this type of input planning would have been unable to transfer resources between goods according to their marginal (weighted) contributions to total revenue. As there is no evidence from the standard instructions issued by Gossnab that enterprises are in fact subject to this detailed control, then the fulfilment of the assortment plan will also depend on the ease and cost of transferring inputs amongst different uses. This is an interesting result as it highlights the 'hidden' importance of the supply plan in ensuring the fulfilment of the assortment plan of the enterprise. A similar conclusion holds in the case of different inputs, x_{11} x_{22}, being used in the production of different goods Q_1 and Q_2:

$$P_1^* \frac{\partial Q_1}{\partial x_{11}} (1 + \lambda_1 + \phi) = \mu_1 + \phi P_1 \qquad (3.34)$$

$$P_2^* \frac{\partial Q_2}{\partial x_{22}} (1 + \lambda_2 + \phi) = \mu_2 + \phi P_2$$

Dividing these two equations

$$\frac{\text{Weighted MRP of input 1 in the production of good 1}}{\text{Weighted MRP of input 2 in the production of good 2}} = \frac{\mu_1 + \phi P_1}{\mu_2 + \phi P_2} \qquad (3.35)$$

Here the maximising condition is that the ratio of the relevant weighted MRPs must equal the weighted relative input prices. Although the expression is cumbersome its economic explanation is straightforward. If the marginal (weighted) contribution to the total revenue per (weighted) kopek spent on buying and using extra amounts of inputs 1 or 2 is different, then total revenue can be increased by switching the expenditure of that kopek not only from one input to another but also from the production of one good to another. The capacity of the enterprise to do so will depend, again, on the degree of detail of input planning, the willingness of the Gossnab to enforce the plans, and the cost of transference of inputs amongst the production of goods.

The analysis has so far abstracted from the cost of transferring the inputs between uses, that is modification, transport and storage costs. Another cost could be expenditures in securing either the connivance of Gossnab officials in illegal exchanges or sales between enterprises or the weak enforcement of the input plan. In the latter case the enterprise may use its own inputs for unauthorised purposes. In either case transferring inputs between uses may incur a cost over and above that of their official prices either because the transference is effectively illegal or because the input needs some modification(12). The cost of transference can now be added to the costs of inputs or subtracted from their MRPs. The results derived from equations (3.32) and (3.34) do not change except that now the switching of inputs from use to use will be limited, especially if the marginal costs of the transference increases. High enough costs will discourage reallocation of inputs altogether as they will tend to cancel out any perceived differences in the MRP of one input between different goods.

The Single Product Model

Horowitz and Martin(13) produced analytical models of the Soviet enterprise that have pushed the discussion much nearer to the post-1965 realities. In the case of Martin's model, a managerial utility function was used that contained as arguments the two sources of funds from which bonuses etc. were derived: The

Models of the Soviet Industrial Enterprise

Material Incentives Fund and the Socio-cultural Fund. The size of these funds depended on the rate of growth of either sales of profits and the level of profitability. Martin's model produced fairly standard neoclassical results concerning input utilization and the level of output, but no comparative statics were attempted. Utilising some of the diagrammatical techniques introduced by Horowitz and Martin, the following is a fairly realistic model of a Soviet enterprise operating in the 1970s.

The maximand of this model will be the level of output. Soviet enterprises are expected to maximise sales subject to constraints. Given however that output prices are fixed, inventories in this one period model are ignored. Since enterprises operate in a seller's market it makes no difference to the analytics of the single-product enterprise where Q or PQ is maximised. The constraints are the input plan and a minimum level of profitability. The price of the good does therefore enter the model via profits. In reality, the targets of the five-year plan are expressed in terms of percentage annual growth of sales, or profitability etc. In this static model it will be assumed that the enterprise in maximising output Q_t will achieve at least Q_{t-1}. A constraint of the form $[Q_t/Q_t - Q_{t-1}] > b$, b being the planned percentage increase in sales is therefore irrelevant. Incorporating a constraint on the minimum increase in labour productivity did not improve the predictive capacity of the model and hence, for the sake of simplicity, it was left out.

The basic outline of the model is as follows

$$\text{Maximise} \quad Q(x_1 \ldots x_n) = \text{output} \tag{3.36}$$

where $Q(\ )$ is the production function assumed to be strictly concave, x_1 is fixed and circulating capital, and $x_2 \ldots x_n$ the rest of the inputs. In order to avoid complex notation both types of capital have been aggregated together. This is not unduly unreal especially in the case of circulating capital which has a precise quantifiable meaning for Soviet enterprises. In addition to this profitability in the real Soviet context is defined in terms of both fixed and circulating capital used (see pp.20-21 of this book for the relevant definitions).

Subject to:

(a) A profitability constraint

$$\frac{\Pi}{P^*x_1} \geqslant R \tag{3.37}$$

where Π is profits and P^* is the cost price of fixed and circulating capital stock and R is the minimum level of profitability. Π is defined as

$$\Pi = P\,Q(x_1 \ldots x_n) - \sum_{i=2}^{n} P_i x_i - P^* x_1 \, r \qquad (3.38)$$

and where r is an interest charge made on the capital used and P is the price of the good produced. The definition of profitability used for part of the tenth FYP was gross i.e. it excluded capital charges. But previous practice seems to have varied and net profitability was also used.   For the sake of simplicity the gross definition is used here, that is

$$PQ(x_1 \ldots x_n) - \sum_{i=2}^{n} P_i x_i \qquad (3.39)$$

Equation (3.37) can now be written as

$$PQ(x_1 \ldots x_n) - \sum_{i=2}^{n} P_i x_i - P^* x_1 R \geqslant 0 \qquad (3.40)$$

Two versions of this model were explored, one with the net the other with the gross profitability definition.   There were no differences at all in the resulting predictions.

(b)   A series of input constraints

$$\bar{X}_1 - x_1 \geqslant 0 \qquad \text{Capital, fixed and circulating}$$

$$\bar{X}_i - x_i \geqslant 0 \qquad \text{Rest of inputs, } i = 2 \ldots m \qquad (3.41)$$

where $\bar{X}_1 \ldots \bar{X}_n$ are the allocated fixed amounts of planned inputs.

These constraints incorporate the input plan of the enterprise as specified by the Gossnab or any other superior agency such as a glavki allocating inputs.   Stocks of inventories carried over from the previous period are not shown explicitly because they can be covered under any other appropriate input heading i.e. stocks of fuel, raw material etc.   There is of course a limit on inventory use because they are finite and depend on input use in the previous period.   As this is a one period model, fluctuations in inventories do not enter the picture.

In the course of the single production cycle examined here some of the inputs constraints may not be binding.   The effect of that on enterprise behaviour will be examined later on when unplanned inputs (i.e. inputs not allocated by or obtained from the Gossnab) will be incorporated explicitly in the models used.

The Lagrangean expression for maximisation is

$$L = Q(x_1 \ldots x_n) + \lambda \left[PQ\,(\ ) - \sum_{i=2}^{n} P_i x_i - P^* x_1 R \right] + \mu_1 \left[\bar{X}_1 - x_1 \right]$$

$$+ \mu_2 \left[\bar{X}_2 - x_2 \right] + \ldots \mu_n \left[\bar{X}_n - x_n \right] \qquad (3.42)$$

where λ and μ are the Lagrangean multipliers indicating the shadow price of the profitability and input plans in terms of the maximand, here the level of output. So, for example, the value of λ would indicate the effect, in terms of output, of a small variation in the profitability plan. A similar interpretation holds for the μs. The usual Kuhn-Tucker conditions for the maximising values of $x_1 \ldots x_n$, λ and $\mu_1 \ldots \mu_n$ were then obtained.

As the number of constraints in this model, $n+1$, exceeds that of the variables, n, at least one of the constraints is redundant. In other words either the profitability or the capital (fixed and circulating) plan or any other input plan will not be binding at the maximising level of the solutions to the Lagrangean expression (3.42). It also follows that if the capital input plan is binding then the profitability constraint becomes a constraint on profits. In other words from equation (3.40) if $x_1 = \bar{X}_1$ then

$$\pi > P * \bar{X}_1 R \qquad\qquad (3.43)$$

the RHS of the inequality being now a fixed number. In undertaking a series of comparative statics exercises it was necessary to make certain assumptions as to which of the constraints were binding at the maximising solution and which were not. Various combinations were tried but none of them produced any conclusive results(14).

A comparative statics exercise on the effects on input utilisation of changes in input plans and prices produced either inconclusive results (indetermined signs) or no responses at all. Several combinations and permutations of binding constraints were used but none of them affected the results. Some of the results obtained are easily interpreted within the mathematical structure of the model. For example increases in the relative price of an input which is being fully utilised within the allocated amount by Gossnab cannot lead to an increase in the use of a substitute input whose constraint is also binding. Increases in the allocation of an input might lead to increases in its use, if this will not affect the profits or profitability constraint, where this is binding. As Portes(15) has commented,

> ... one must begin to question the marginal utility of further exercises of this kind ... I wonder whether the problems with which a model like this can deal with are really the important ones. How much significance, for example, can we attribute to the new incentives system, when it has been introduced in the hardly unchanged context of an administratively controlled economy with the material technical supply fully operating, prices inflexible etc?

This might be an unduly pessimistic view of the matter however.

FIGURE 3.4   Sales maximisation and increases in capital

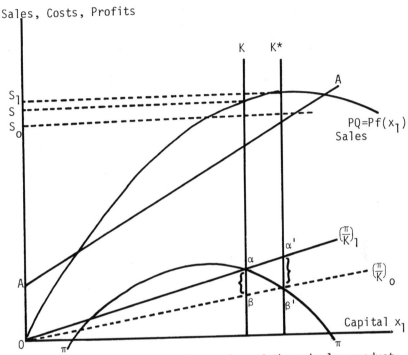

A more complex diagrammatical version of the single product
model outlined above did permit a useful insight and explanation of the comparative static results.   In Figure 3.4
the level of output is expressed as a function of fixed and circulating capital x_1.   The rest of the inputs $x_2 \ldots x_n$ are
assumed to be constant. The marginal productivity of capital
declines as the intensity of its use increases, hence the shape
and slope of the $Q = f(x_1)$ curve. Physical output can be turned
into ruble values by multiplying Q with the fixed output price
P and continuing to use the assumption that all output is sold.
The vertical axis of Figure 3.4 now plots ruble values including
those of sales.
     Curve AA shows total cost of production as a function of
the cost of capital employed rP^*x_1. Since both P^* and r are
constant, AA is a straight line.   Given that the rest of the
inputs $x_2 \ldots x_n$ are assumed to be fixed then the outlays in
their purchase and use are also fixed and equal to OA.   Making
output a function of capital only is not unrealistic in the context of the comparative statics exercise about to be undertaken
and is also convenient as it allows us to express profitability
in terms of the capital used. The total profits curve ππ is
derived by subtracting AA from PQ. Profits here are net since

71

the cost of using capital is subtracted from the revenue. The enterprise is allocated $K = P*\bar{X}_1$ amount of capital; if now the minimum sales (output) plan is S, and the minimum planned profitability is $(\Pi/K)_1$, then from a micro consistency point of view the plan is feasible and the enterprise can fulfil all its targets without breaching any of the plans. It is of course assumed that the allocation of $x_2 \ldots x_n$ inputs is sufficient so that in combination with $P*\bar{X}_1$, the $S = PQ$ plan can be achieved.

Should the capital input allocation plan increase to $K*$ then, ceteris paribus, the enterprise can increase its sales to S_1 but in the process of doing so it will breach the profitability constraint by an amount equal to $\alpha'\beta'$. If the original profitability constraint was $(\Pi/K)_0$ and the minimum sales plan S_0 then the enterprise, before the increase in the capital allocation, would have been overfulfilling its plans by $S_1 - S_0$ and $\alpha\beta$. Even in the case where the two constraints were not effective, there is no a priori reason to believe that an increase in capital allocation will either increase capital utilisation or output if:

(a)   That might entail a fall of profitability to say $(\Pi/K)_0$ or a decrease of the overfulfilment of the profitability target i.e. any level between $(\Pi/K)_1$ and $(\Pi/K)_0$.
(b)   It could possibly reduce the degree of the fulfilment of the sales target. This could have been the case if the increase in the capital allocation was bigger than $K*$.

It follows that to predict the results of the comparative static analysis will require a specification of the managerial utility function and the relevant bonus scheme.

Figure 3.5 explores the comparative statics results of increasing either the cost price of capital $P*$ or cost of its use r. The curve AA will swivel upwards to AA' and the profits curve will fall to $\Pi'\Pi'$. Similar results can be obtained by increasing the cost of the fixed inputs $x_2 \ldots x_n$ in which case AA will shift upwards parallel to itself. If the original inputs, sales and profitability plans were exactly fulfilled prior to the increase in the cost price of capital, i.e. S of sales, (Π/K) of profitability and K amount of capital utilized, then the enterprise will be faced with the following options:

(a)   It may reduce sales to S_0 in order to maintain the level of profitability at Π/K by using K_0 of capital.
(b)   It may maintain sales at S at the expense of the profitability plan (now underfulfilled by $\alpha\beta$).
(c)   It may resort to a combination of (a) and (b).

The outcome again depends on the relative weight attached by the managers of the enterprise to the different goals. In addition to this, the degree of input substitution and therefore the tautness of the input plan may prove crucial in determining the

FIGURE 3.5   Sales maximization and increases in costs

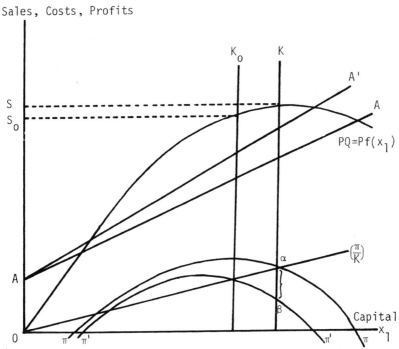

outcome.   Similar exercises can be carried out with a variety of combinations of constraints some of which are binding
and others not, with equally ambiguous results.   In the final
analysis 'many maximands are no maximand'(16).

3.4 SOVIET MODELS OF THE ENTERPRISE: A BRIEF SUMMARY

Soviet microeconomic modelling of enterprises is still relatively underdeveloped as compared to the extensive research and
literature on macroeconomic models. One suspects that undue
attention to independent patterns of behaviour of units subject
to the guidance of planners might cast an unfavourable light on
the ability of planners to direct and control them.   This is
not reflected however in the voluminous literature on the role
and effectiveness of bonus schemes, as opposed to straight
'models of the firm', and the role of enterprises in the reformed
economy. And herein lies an interesting contradiction.   The
greater the emphasis on bonus and incentive schemes, the more the
silent, implicit acceptance by Soviet planners that managers and
enterprises can and do behave independently of the planners'
wishes.   This must be so, otherwise the incentive schemes would

not be necessary if managers simply did as they were told.
Katz, commenting on the post-1965 era, summarised this basic
contradiction thus(17):

> For other aspects of the political significance of the
> reform one must examine the systematic changes that have
> taken place and are likely to follow. In the first place
> the principle is now established that the enterprise is
> the basic operating cell of all the economy. Of course
> these words are not new. They were as a matter of fact
> used in the Stalin organisational reforms at the begin-
> ning of the first FYP to distinguish the enterprise from
> the trust and to establish the authority of the non-
> khozraschetny governmental regime. But now the emphasis
> seems clearly to be on the assertion of enterprise
> rights with respect to the governmental administration
> ... The principle of enterprise rights acts in the
> direction of an erosion of totalitarian control since
> it establishes an independence of action of lower units
> vis-a-vis hierarchical organizations of the state ...
> But the urge to atomize and control proved far stronger
> than the desire for spontaneous creative initiative in
> harmony with the ruling will, simply because of the
> fear that such initiative would not be in harmony.

Like in the case of the role of suppliers in general and the
Gossnab in particular, Soviet authors tend to deal with the details
but occasionally bypass some of the interesting contradictions
of institutions pulling, in several instances, to opposite
directions.

The cause of this relative underdevelopment of analysis
cannot be either attributed to ignorance, since neoclassical
microeconomic techniques are familiar to Soviet mathematical
economists. A more likely explanation is that Soviet economists
might have tried and abandoned early on the neoclassical model
(for reasons that by now must be amply apparent) and concentrated
instead on more practical aspects of enterprise behaviour. The
outcome of this is a mixed bag of models, some of which concentrate exclusively on numerical/empirical aspects others being
purely descriptive and lacking any basic behavioural assumptions.

These models can be, crudely, classified under three categories. Firstly, straight linear programming modes, emphasi-
sing the practicality of the technique and serving purely
utilitarian functions, namely rescheduling of production capacity, changes in inputs use etc. Secondly, accounting-descrip-
tive models which consist mainly of a number of accounting
identities and equations describing aspects of the operations
of the enterprise. Actual data or experimental values are then
introduced in the model and the outcome or prediction is then
used to explore possible ways of improving planning methods and
techniques. Finally, a hybrid type of model which shows the

greatest promise for further and meaningful modelling of the Soviet enterprise consists of both accounting equations and identities but underpinned by maximising or minimising assumptions. Variables are usually estimated by using econometric techniques and both experimental and actual data are then introduced and used for sensitivity analysis. This may include comparing the predictions made by the model under different assumptions or with parameters changed with the actual outcome. It may also involve comparing the planned predictions of performance with the predictions of the model and drawing some operationally significant conclusions from these.

A typical example of the first type of model can be found in Popof(18) where a series of linear programming models are applied to various aspects of operations of enterprises in sugar, oil refinery, paper making and silk weaving. The objective functions involved either maximisation of output or minimising costs subject to input or output constraints. Most of the models were solved numerically. In the case, for example, of silk weaving the aim was to minimise loom costs subject to a minimum output. The numerical solution led to a reorganisation of allocation of output amongst the enterprises of the relevant association with a subsequent fall in the cost of production of about 3%. A similar exercise applied a linear programming model to data from machine tool enterprises. The aim was to maximise profits subject to twelve constraints which included capacity limitation, factor productivities and to carry out a sensitivity analysis on the level of output product and gross or net profits(19). The second type of model can assume various forms, sometimes merging into the third type. A common approach to this area of modelling is exemplified in the work of Bagrinovskii and Yegorova(20). They set out a model of the enterprise in purely accounting identity forms, introduce certain parameters that can be changed, and on that basis carry out what amounts to primitive comparative statics exercises. The latter expression is not quite accurate as most of these models avoid any behavioural assumptions (i.e. maximisation of profits etc.) but look at the operations of the enterprise from a mechanistic point of view. Although these models are interesting for the microeconomic data they may contain (a truly rare animal in Soviet statistics - except in anecdotal form) they still miss the basic ingredient of a true model - testable predictions.

The basic elements of the Bagrinovskii-Yegorova model are as follows: The actual and potential output of the enterprise is expressed as a proportional function of its capital stock and equipment. The aim of the model is to try to explore the conditions under which the planned and actual levels of output will coincide. So, for example, if the maximum capacity of the plant is N and the achieved capacity is N* then the planned output Q_p can be either $Q_p > N$ or $Q_p < N$. In the latter case the plan may well have been either $Q_p > N*$ or $Q_p < N*$. The achieved capacity can, of course, be influenced by parameters such as the

Models of the Soviet Industrial Enterprise

level of material incentives funds (MIF) or the funds for the
development of production. An index measuring the importance
of these funds in influencing labour productivity and the
potential reduction in costs of economising materials (both
being fund-forming indexes) is constructed along the following
lines:

For labour productivity

$$d = 1 + a(1 - e^{-x_1})$$

For economising in the use of materials:

$$n = 1 - b(1 - e^{-x_2})$$

where x_1 and x_2 are defined as

$$x_1 = (1 - k)MIF/WF \qquad \text{and} \quad x_2 = kMIF/WF$$

with a, b and k being given norms, WF being the wages fund and
MIF the material incentives fund. It now follows that the minimum value of the indexes d and n will be 1 when $x_1 = x_2 = 0$. As
x_1 and x_2 approach infinity then $d \to (1 + a)$ and $n \to (1 - b)$.
These two indexes are then used to measure the degree of
increase if the efficiency of capital utilisation (for example
the movement of the incremental output/capital ratio) and the
length of the production cycle. The idea is that the existence
of the incentive funds will affect the overall efficiency of the
enterprise and therefore these specific measurements of performance. Several purely accounting definitions of costs and
profitability are then entered into the actual formulas used to
derive the incentive funds. So for example for the MIF:

$$MIF_{planned} = WF \; \alpha\beta \left[\left[\left(\frac{Q_a - Q_p}{Q_p} \right) \right] \right] + \gamma\varepsilon(R_a - R_p)$$

where α, β, γ, ε, are norms depending on whether the plan is
over or under fulfilled, Q and R are output and profitability
and the subscripts a and p refer to actual or planned. The
model is now in a sense closed. Actual numbers are then introduced in the accounting relationships and the behaviour of the
enterprise can be simulated. A kind of comparative statics
can also be obtained by varying the parameter values and observing the resulting differences between the actual and planned
targets.

Finally, the third type of models may also assume various
forms; a hybrid version of this kind of model is exemplified
in an article by Bromberg et al.(21). Using eighteen annual
observations from the operation of an All-Union industrial
association, the authors tried to predict the behaviour of key

variables such as costs of production, profits, capital accumulation etc. over the 1973-1990 period and compare the future predicted performance of the association with its performance so far. The model for example predicted that costs would rise in the future much faster than they had done in the past with a consequent squeeze on the profit margin per rouble value of output. The actual quantitative findings are not interesting per se, as they can only acquire any kind of economic significance by comparing them with what actually did happen in 1973-1990. The methodology of the exercise however is interesting.

A production function of the following form was used

$$Y_t = aL^b K_1^c K_2^d e^{vt}$$

where Y is output, L is labour, K_1 and K_2 fixed and circulating capital, e^{vt} an exponential function allowing for technical progress, a, b, c, d and v, were fixed coefficients. Several accounting expression for profits, deductions from profits directed towards the incentives funds, capital formation etc. were then defined. Econometric calculation of the coefficients allowed for partial quantification of the equations. The value of this model is limited as there were no behavioural elements in it allowing for prediction and explanation of the behaviour of the enterprises over time.

Two relatively recent models both based on the operations of enterprises in petrochemical engineering must also be mentioned. Belkin and Pomanskii(22) concentrated on the role of profits and prices as links that can be used to coordinate the aims of the planners and those of the enterprise. The enterprise is assumed to maximise profits subject to an inputs constraint. The maximising values thus obtained were then compared to the actual planned targets. This helped to highlight a number of interesting points, such as the affect of prices on profitability, and also yielded a number of recommendations concerning possible price changes so as to influence the behaviour of the enterprise. A considerably more complex model was developed by Belkin et al.(23) focusing on the factors influencing the degree of fulfilment of planned targets. A combination of accounting equations and definitions plus econometric estimation of a number of variables was used to examine the accuracy by which the model predicted the behaviour of enterprises as witnessed by the comparison with actual performance. In most cases the degree of divergence was less than 1 percent. A simulation exercise was then undertaken by assuming that the enterprise was attempting to maximise total output in physical units, total sales and average wages plus bonuses per worker. The predicted maximising values were then compared to actual data. Some interesting, albeit not unexpected, results were obtained. For example it emerged that it was much easier for the enterprise concerned to fulfil its planned output in value rather than physical terms thus throwing, again, in sharp relief

Models of the Soviet Industrial Enterprise

the problem of setting appropriate prices.

There is a common characteristic amongst the Soviet models surveyed: their direct and practical approach to enterprise behaviour. There is a problem however that until recently, plagued Soviet econometric and quantitative research on industrial enterprises and that was testing without a theory. This will become particularly apparent when some Soviet econometric evidence on the appraisal of bonus schemes is examined in Chapter 6. Models however like the last two ones outlined above indicate that Soviet researchers are now giving greater prominence to the concepts of behavioural assumptions in setting up their models. So far Soviet researchers appear to have avoided the rather sterile exercises of their western counterparts in modelling the Soviet enterprise possibly because they have direct access to raw microeconomic data, which is almost totally lacking in western research. A point of convergence however is emerging in the Soviet and western approaches to the modelling of the Soviet enterprise, centred around the attempts to construct models that yield testable predictions.

Notes

1. M. Feshbach, 'Manpower Management', Problems of Communism. Nov.-Dec. 1974, p.23.
2. D. Ward, The Socialist Economy, Random House, New York 1967, pp.84-101 and Ch.7 passim and his contribution 'The Planner's Choice Variables' in G. Grossman (Ed.), Value and Plan, University of California Press, Berkeley 1960, pp.132-161.
3. B. Balassa, 'La Theorie de la Firm Socialiste', in Economie Applique, Oct.-Dec. 1959, pp.535-70.
4. See Ekonomicheskaya Gazeta No.50, Dec. 1976, Supplement p.3, where reference is made on the differentiation of fund-forming indexes depending on the 'glavnykh zadach' i.e. departmental tasks, of the different departments, associations, enterprises etc. Although this reference does not make explicit what these problems or tasks are, they may well include an attempt to minimise planned losses by allowing for differences in costs. The author, however, has found no evidence of this differential applied in practice or any explicit justification for their possible application.
5. E. Ames, Soviet Economic Processes, R.D. Irwin, Illinois 1965, Ch.4, passim.

6. Berliner, The Innovation Decision in Soviet Industry, Part II passim.

7. D.W. Conclin, An Evaluation of the Soviet Profit Reforms, Praeger, New York 1970, Ch.7 passim.

8. J.P. Bonin, 'On Soviet Managerial Incentives Structures', Southern Economic Journal, Vol.42, No.3, Jan. 1976, pp.490-495.

9. See also a useful but short summary in T. Buck, Comparative Industrial Systems, Macmillan, London 1982, pp.47-55.

10. A. Zaubermann, Aspects of Planometrics, Athlone Press, London 1967, pp.115-135.

11. The assumption of independent production functions is based on the following premises.

Firstly, interdependent production functions could be introduced into this model by assuming that some of the goods are jointly produced, i.e. the quantities of two or more outputs are technically interdependent - the mutton/wool, hides/beef type of case. In the simplest case of two outputs being produced by the use of one input, the rate of product transformation will be equal to the ratio of the marginal products of the input used in the production. Similar conclusions would hold for the multiproduct, multi-input case. Deriving product transformation equations does assume that the enterprise is free to vary the output mix. In the case of joint products two asumptions can be made. One is that the enterprise is expected to produce the goods in question in fixed proportions say $Q_1/Q_2 =$ K. In this case it is possible to construct a composite good consisting of K units of Q_2 and one unit of Q_2 and then apply the analysis of the single product firm. The other assumption however, and more relevantly in the case of the Soviet enterprise is, that the firm might be expected to produce minimum quantities of Q_1 and Q_2 rather than fixed proportions. The analysis of the multiproduct and multi-input firm becomes very complex in this case because some of the goods would be jointly produced but others not. Hence the model would need to specify separate production functions for joint and non-jointly produced goods adding greatly to the complexity. If the enterprise however is assumed to produce some goods jointly but in fixed proportions (a crude assortment plan), then these goods can be aggregated together and treated as one output. This assumption does no great injury to realism but allows the specification of separate production functions for the rest of the goods and individual production functions for the composite (jointly produced) outputs.

Secondly, the standard references on the multiproduct multi-input firm always specify separate production functions for each good. The use of transformation functions runs into problems because of the inequality constraints used here. Purely interdependent functions other than the special case of jointly produced goods involve the presence of externalities, an important but irrelevant consideration here.

Models of the Soviet Industrial Enterprise

In the final analysis the degree of unreality of certain assumptions must be judged against the predictions that single models afford. The basic references on the multi-input multi-output firm are:

(a) R.W. Pfouts, 'The Theory of Cost and Production in the Multi-product Firm', Econometrica, Vol.29, Oct. 1961, pp.650-658.

(b) R.S. Pfouts, 'Multi-product Firms vs Single Product Firms, The Theory of Cost and Production. Metroeconomica, May-Aug. 1964, pp.51-66.

(c) C.E. Ferguson, The Neoclassical Theory of Production and Distribution, Cambridge University Press, Cambridge 1969, Ch.10.

12. If the model being used here was extended to cover the case of a sector rather than one multiproduct enterprise then a set of similar equations to (3.34) would apply for inter-enterprise transfers, if that was possible under the Gossnab rules. That possibility, however, would imply some form of an inputs market with the costs of the tolkatchi ('pushers' or unofficial arrangers that expedite deliveries and in general break through the bureaucratic barriers), representing the premium over and above the Gosplan-Gossnab fixed price.

13. B. Horowitz, 'Profit Responsibility in Soviet Enter-prises', Journal of Business of University of Chicago, Jan. 1968, pp.47-55. J.M. Martin, Reforms and the Maximizing Behaviour of the Soviet Firm in J. Thorton (Ed.), Economic Analysis of the Soviet-Type Systems, Cambridge University Press, Cambridge 1977, pp.216-241.

14. If at the maximising solution some of the constraints are binding and all the inputs are used then some of the in-equalities of the maximising conditions will be equations. The bordered Hessian is a determinant of $(2n+1) \times (2n+1)$ order. Given that some of the constraints will be redundant here, the maxi-mum number that can be binding and allowing at the same time the signing of the comparative statics results, is n-1. This is found as follows. In order to sign the results it is necessary to start with the $2(n+1)+1 = 2n+3$ principal minor alternating in sign according to $(-1)(m+1)+1=m+2$ sequence. A principal minor of the order 2n+3 is of course bigger than the bordered deter-minant itself which is 2n+1. The solution here is to assume that any two constraints are not binding, say $\mu_{n-1} = \mu_n = 0$. The Hessian will then be of $(2n-1) \times (2n-1)$ order and the principal minor of $2(n-1) + 1 = (2n-1)$ order as well thus allowing the signing of the comparative static results.

15. R. Portes in a commentary on an earlier draft of J.M. Martin's paper. My thanks to Prof. Portes for letting me have a copy of his comments.

16. P. Wiles, Economic Institutions Compared, Basil Blackwell, Oxford 1977, p.82.

17. A. Katz, The Politics of Economic Reform in the Soviet Union, Praeger, New York 1972, pp.191-92.

80

18. I.G. Popof (Ed.), Matematicheskie metody v planirovanii otraslei i predpriyatii, Moscow, 1973 passim, but esp.
pp.160, 162.
19. R.P. Sheinman, 'Optimizatsia proizvodstvennoi progra-
mmy predpriyatii i obyedinenii', in Ekonomika i Matematicheskie
Metody, Vol.10, No.3, 1974.
20. K.A. Bagrinovskii and I.E. Yegorova, Ekonomiko-
matimaticheskaya model' khozraschetnogo promyshlenogo predpri-
yatia. In the volume Mathematicheski voprosy formirovanya
ekonomicheskikh modely, edited by E. Berland, Moscow 1973, pp.
83-96.
21. G.L. Bromberg, N.I. Buzova, G.B. Kleiner, 'O Modeli
ekonomicheskoi deyatel'nosti khozraschetnogo promyshlennogo
obyedineniya' in Ekonomika i Matematicheskie Metody, Vol.10, No.
2, 1974, pp.303-314.
22. M. Belkin and A. Pomanskii, "Model' ekonomicheskogo
stimulirovaniya vypolneniya plana proizvodstva' in Ekonomika i
Matematicheskie Metody, Vol.17, 1981, No.3, pp.584-592.
23. M. Belkin, V. Volkonskii et al., 'Modelirovaniye
vozdeistviya khozyaistvennogo mekhanizma na pokazateli raboty
predpriyatiya' in Ekonomika i Matematicheskie Metody, Vol.16,
No.5, 1980, pp.880-892. See also translations of this article in
Matekon, Winter 1981-82, pp.32-51.

Chapter Four

PLAN TAUTNESS AND ENTERPRISE BEHAVIOUR

4.1 INTRODUCTION

The discussion so far of the models of Soviet enterprise has left out one specific dimension of both the economic and institutional framework within which enterprises operate: the problem of plan tautness. The role, measurement and effects of tautness have recently acquired additional importance. The quasi-parametric methods that Soviet planners have had to use to control enterprises are now directed to bonus systems that are supposed to encourage managers to put forward plans that reflect the true capacity of the enterprise and at the same time eliminate the problem of the ratchet effect of high achievement. So both the definition, measurement and quantitative significance of planned tautness has become an area of concern and research for planners.

This chapter explores the different interpretations of tautness in both the Soviet and western literature and summarises the available empirical evidence on the effect of tautness. The approaches to this issue are examined separately and their predictions or interpretations of Soviet planning practice are noted. A penultimate section summarises critically the findings and compares them against empirical evidence. Finally the conclusions and the implications for the further analysis of the Soviet enterprise are set out and related to the material presented in the following chapters.

4.2 THE ANALYTICS OF TAUTNESS

Tautness is the relationship between the plan enterprises are expected to fulfil and their productive capacity or inputs allocated to them. The greater the difference between what planners expect or believe the enterprises can achieve and what they can actually do, the greater the degree of tautness.

Tautness can arise either by design or error. There are several sub-groupings and cases that can be identified under these two broad headings.

Firstly, tautness can arise as the result of a deliberate act on the part of the planners in putting forward plans they know cannot be fulfilled, in the hope of extorting either hidden reserves and productive capacity from the enterprise or having a psychological effect on the recipients of the plan. This approach was first explored and formalised by Hunter in terms of the 'hortatory effects' of taut planning in the Soviet Union(1).

Secondly, tautness may arise as the result of uncertainty over the specific production function of different industries and sectors. The planners may be guessing at the true capacity of the enterprise and hence over-estimate it. The errors here might not be purely random, because, the degree of uncertainty will change over time as more information becomes available on the behaviour and productive capacity of the enterprise. In that case, as the planners are becoming aware of the true extent of the productive capacity of the enterprise, the tautness in the plan may well be defined as hortatory. This highlights the difficulty of attempting a clear-cut classification of the types of causes of plan tautness. This approach has received considerable attention by western authors, especially in relation to bonus schemes that encouraged overfulfilment of targets. The role of the bonus schemes is related to the hortatory aspects of tautness since moral pressure may be accompanied by financial incentives to overfulfil. In both the first and the second approaches outlined so far there is an underlying assumption of an optimum degree of tautness, i.e. a level of pressure that at the margin equalizes the beneficial and dysfunctional effects of higher planned targets. The main contributor in this area was Keren(2).

The availability of reserves, but of an unplanned kind, was the subject of a third approach to this area by Portes(3). His model was non-stochastic and concentrated on the effects of varying tautness rather than the causes of it. Tautness in this model is defined in purely supply terms. The availability of inputs over and above those planned by Gosplan and distributed by Gossnab would indicate a loosely enforced input plan. Complete tautness in the input plan is signified by the non-availability of these unplanned inputs.

Fourthly Wiles(4) has suggested that tension can be produced by bonus schemes that encouraged overfulfilment:

> With or without a taut plan the manager will certainly make everything taut if his livelihood depends on it, and overfulfilment is held to be virtue and rewarded. This reward is of course independent of anybody's success in actually marketing the extra output ... So managers have every interest in high bonuses for overfulfilment with low tension ...

It would now follow that tension would vary directly with the degree of emphasis, backed by money, that the bonus schemes laid on overfulfilment. The tautness generated here would feed through the system via excessive input demands and low output plans submitted by enterprises and the subsequent reaction of planners in increasing output plans and reducing input allocation.

Finally, tautness could arise out of pure error or incompetency on the part of the planners. This is a tempting proposition given the magnitude of the tasks facing Soviet planners. There is a serious problem here in that tautness is associated with plans which are impossible or very difficult to fulfil. If plans are persistently underfulfilled over a long period of time because of errors, then it would appear that planners do not learn from their mistakes and that they err consistently in one direction. To put it crudely, it is unlikely that a Gosplan-Gossnab typist over a forty-year period would make the same mistake in omitting a zero from the input allocation and adding to the output plan! The error interpretation of tautness would be interesting if the incidence of over and underfulfilment (i.e. planners erring on the side of slackness as well as tautness) was randomly distributed. The statistical evidence presented at the end of this chapter points to the opposite direction.

In examining all these different versions of how tautness is generated, it is important to note that almost invariably the concept relates to performance with respect to planned output. For example the process of 'storming' i.e. a final almost desperate attempt to fulfil planned targets at the end of the appropriate time period (month, quarter etc.) may squeeze some more output from the enterprise. Profit or cost reduction targets, however, cannot be 'stormed'. It is true, of course, that planners can and do set high or unrealistic targets for any planned target thus pushing the capacity of the enterprise to, say, cut costs or increase profits to the limit. In these cases tautness may acquire a different meaning. For the rest of the section the analysis will concentrate primarily on the effects of tautness on output. A somewhat different approach will be taken in dealing with the degree of tautness as evidenced in the input plan and on the availability of unplanned input supplies for the enterprise.

4.3 EFFORT AND UNCERTAINTY

Hunter's original treatment of the question of tautness was briefly this: increases in the output plan in relation to inputs may lead to underfulfilment. This in itself is not undesirable, because, if the pressure exerted on the enterprise results to an increase in output which would not have occurred otherwise then the underfulfilment can be justified. There is therefore a potential relationship between planned increases in

output and actual increases in output.   What causes that
relationship to exist at all may well be the outcome of a bonus
system that encourages enterprises to bring forth hidden reserves
as tautness increases or might be what Hunter calls hortatory
effects of taut planning.
     In Figure 4.1 the TT curve shows the postulated relationship
between plan and the actual outcome. Low percentage increases
result to plan overfulfilment, with high percentage planned increases leading eventually to underfulfilment.   Hunter's argument is that planners may rationally try for planned increases
of B as opposed to A precisely because the additional output
produced justified the underfulfilment.   It then follows that
there is a particular percentage increase in targets that is
optimising the relationship between the degree of underfulfilment and the additional output produced.

FIGURE 4.1   Relationship between planned and actual output

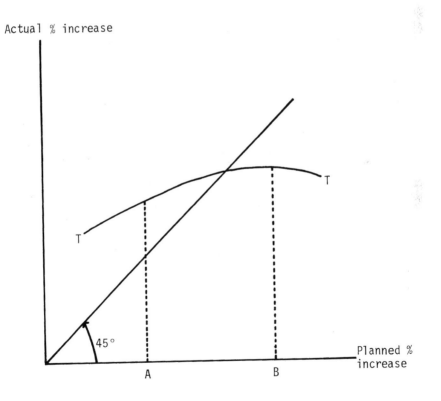

FIGURE 4.2   Optimum tautness

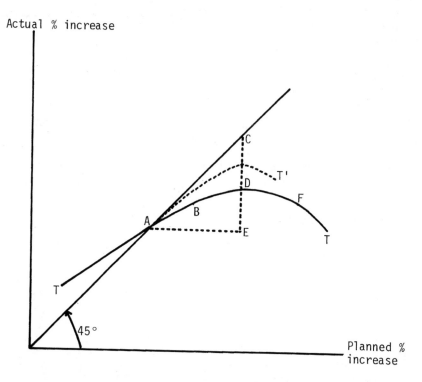

Actual % increase

Planned % increase

In Figure 4.2 at point B the actual increases in performance will still fall short of the planned target. The distance
from the 45° line to point B shows the estimated strength of the
dysfunctional forces. These forces can be defined in terms of
developing bottlenecks, equipment breakdown because of poor
maintenance, higher rejection rates as quality falls and, of
course, growing physical, mental and psychological fatigue of
the workers and managers. A point such as F would indicate a
percentage increase in the plans that is too taut in the sense
that if the plan was reduced then there would be an increase in
the actual percentage growth, say to D.   The crucial point in
Hunter's analysis lies in the definition of the degree of planned increases that just about balance any losses resulting from
too taut a plan. At point D in Figure 4.2 the dysfunctional
forces equal the gains from demanding more production, i.e. CD
= DE. For levels of targets to the right of A the gains out-
weigh the losses whilst to the right of D the dysfunctional
forces dominate the situation. In Hunter's own words:

    ... Plan targets should be increased up to the point
    where losses from overtautness exactly match   the

> estimated gains from ambitious target increases. This
> is evidently a general operating principle of consider-
> able importance. It shows for example that dysfunctional
> features of a growth program should not be reduced to
> zero. As long as they are associated with tautness
> that is pulling the system forward their negative in-
> fluence can be sustained up to the level of gains that
> justify them.   ('Optimal Tautness ...', p.566)

Hunter's rule in its simplest states that increases in
targets should continue up to AE percent increase in Figure
4.2 because here the percentage underfulfilment CD equals the
percentage gain in output DE caused by the AE percent increase
in plans.
   It is important at this stage to point out that there is a
serious error in Hunter's definition of 'optimising' tautness
concerning the CE = DE rule. In Figure 4.2 the TT curve could
have been redrawn as TT' with the optimum level of tautness in
terms of the percentage planned increase in targets still remaining the same. It then follows that Hunter's definition of
CD = DE is not general enough. It can perhaps be redefined along
the lines that as long as a X% increase in plans elicits a positive (non-zero) increase in actual performance it is worth
maintaining and increasing the planned pressure.   When the
actual response is negative or zero then the pressure should
cease.
   The operational significance of this rule is likely to be
limited. As the structure of the economy and of the bonus
schemes changes, the shape and position of the TT curve will also
change. In the long run successive increases in planned targets may eventually reduce the hortatory effectiveness of tautness as apathy and cynicism set in the management of the enterprise. Hunter's contribution was useful in stimulating research
on the concept of optimum plan tautness. It also reinterpreted
the efforts of pre-war Soviet planners in terms of an attempt
to exploit the positive rather than dysfunctional forces of
taut planning.
   Keren developed a similar model in the sense that the
tautness of plans could affect the actual outcome by increasing
the level of effort exerted by the management and staff. The
interesting aspect of Keren's model was that the introduction
of uncertainty in the production side of the enterprise's acti-
vities produced similar results to those derived by Hunter. If
there was no stochastic elements entering the enterprise's
objective function then optimum tautness in plans was defined
on points along the 45° line.
   Keren assumes that all the inputs of the enterprise are
constant except a labour augmenting input which he calls
exertion:

For any expenditure of labour time, the effectiveness

of labour will grow as the workers' exertion increases
... How well an enterprise is run depends a great deal
not only on the innate and acquired ability of the management but also on the effort they put into their work.
('On the Tautness of Plans', p.470)

Keren defines a production function $Q = G(X)$ where Q is
output and X is exertion. All other inputs are assumed to be
constant. Managers are assumed to be maximising their utilities
which are functions of X and C. C is the potential salary and
bonus receivable by the managers and is defined as

$$C = y + b$$

where y is the basic salary and b is the bonus received if
$Q > Q_p$, Q_p being the planned level of output. If $Q < Q_p$ then
$C = y$ only. The utility function of the managers is defined as:

$$U = U(X,C) \text{ with } U_x \leqslant 0 \text{ and } U_c > 0.$$

Keren assumes that if $X = 0$, that is even if there is no
exertion, then $Q > 0$. He then proves that, given the utility
function and the bonus system, as long as the additional utility
attached to additional bonuses is just about equal to the disutility of additional exertion (i.e. over what is necessary to
achieve planned output) then actual and planned outputs will be
the same. This in effect implies that pressure on resources,
i.e. taut planning, will not have any effect on actual output
if the bonus system is not such as to compensate for the extra
effort. This result depends of course on the assumption that
the extra exertion brought about by the bonus system will bring
forth the necessary output, even if the inputs allocated are
not sufficient to do so on the basis of the production function
of the enterprise as perceived by the planners. There is however
a minimum exertion level $(X = 0)$ and a maximum one, both corres-
ponding to some positive level of output. If the planned output
is less than the level of output associated with nil exertion,
or if it is bigger than that associated with the maximum level
of exertion, then the actual level of output will not be affected by the planned level of output. Tautness will not result
in increases in output.

In Figure 4.3 if the planned output is less than Q_A then
the actual output will be Q_1, that is the level of output associated with nil exertion. If planned output is bigger than
Q_A then as long as additional exertion is compensated by the
bonus system in such a way as to equal the disutility of the
extra exertion then planned and actual output will be the same.
If planned output is bigger than Q_B Keren claims that the exertion necessary to achieve this will be bigger than the additional
utility that the bonus will bring and actual output will fall
back to Q_1. This is totally unrealistic. Managers faced with
high percentage increases in their plans will not opt for a very

FIGURE 4.3   Tautness and effort

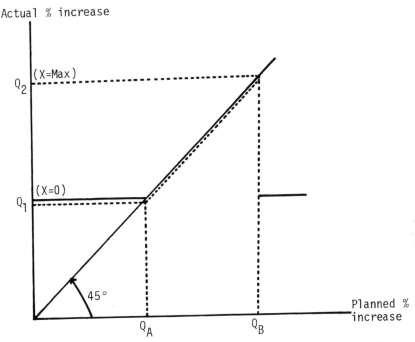

Actual % increase

high percent underfulfilment, i.e. the difference between Q_B and Q_1, just because the bonuses will not compensate them for their efforts. The loss of moral and non-pecuniary incentives may be an important enough consideration to ensure that the actual output does not fall all the way back to Q_1. The point however that Keren is making is that under a given system of bonuses it may not be true that taut plans will bring forth ad- ditional output in the manner described by Hunter.

Uncertainty was introduced in this model by adding a ran- dom variable θ to the production function:

$$Q = G(X + \theta) \quad \text{with } \theta \text{ having } f(\theta) \text{ density function.} \quad (4.1)$$

Managers are expected to have some prior idea about the distri- bution of θ which they express in a subjective probabilistic distribution. This stochastic variable could stand, for example, for suppliers' deliveries whose time of arrival is uncertain. Managers are assumed to be utility maximisers; their utility depends on money, (bonuses), and exertion. It now follows that their utility will increase as output increases which then gen- erates additional income via the bonus scheme.   Increases in exertion however cause disutility. The presence of the stochastic

89

variable in the production function means that increase in exertion necessary to increase output may not be compensated by increases in bonuses. In a more general sense the result of additional exertion is uncertain, since the managers' efforts in trying to secure higher output might be frustrated by non-delivery of inputs. So the stochastic element, and the assumption which Keren does not make explicit, that managers are risk averters, means that the utility attached to the additional bonuses earned will decrease.

Keren uses the trade-off between the disutility of exertion and the utility of money (bonuses) to define the optimum level of exertion for a given bonus scheme. Managers are assumed to maximise their utility $U = U(X,C)$ with C and X defined as previously. C depends on Q but Q now depends on the stochastic variable θ thus making the bonus element of managerial income uncertain. Managers therefore maximise their expected utility

$$E(U) = \int_{\underline{\theta}}^{\bar{\theta}} U(X,C) f(\theta) \, d\theta \tag{4.2}$$

There is a minimum value of θ which will allow enough output Q to be produced so that the plan will be fulfilled. Call that value of θ, θ^*, so that $\underline{\theta} < \theta^* < \bar{\theta}$ where $\underline{\theta}$ and $\bar{\theta}$ are the limiting values of $f(\theta)$. Integrating equation (4.2) gives

$$E(U) = U(X,y) F(\theta^*) + U(X, y+b) \left[1 - F(\theta^*) \right] \tag{4.3}$$

with $F(\theta)$ being the distribution function of $f(\theta)$.

The first expression on the RHS of (4.3) gives the expected value of the utility to the manager of just fulfilling the plan and receiving the minimum income y. The second expression gives the expected value of the utility of producing more than the planned level of output and therefore receiving y plus the bonus b. Maximising (4.3) with respect to X and rearranging:

$$-E \left(\frac{\partial U}{\partial X} \right) = \left[U(X, y+b) - U(X,y) \right] f(\theta^*) \tag{4.4}$$

This expression can be interpreted as follows. The expected disutility of a marginal increment in effort, the LHS of equation (4.4), should equal the expected utility accruing from it, the RHS. That additional expected utility consists of the difference in the utility of bonuses resulting from just over-fulfilling the plan and the utility of just fulfilling the plan and receiving the minimum income y.

The way in which this model was then related to plan tautness was to estimate an optimum target, given the bonus scheme, that would maximise effort and therefore actual output. As plans increased past the optimum target, exertion decreased and so did output. The result is intuitively obvious but the usefulness of Keren's model lies in the predictions as to what

90

happens to both the optimum targets and effort, and therefore, to actual output as uncertainty increased. This was explored by increasing the spread of the density function $f(\theta)$. As uncertainty increased, both the optimum target, that is the plan that would induce maximum effort, and the level of effort declined. Managers are assumed to be utility maximisers but they also attach decreasing utility to additional uncertain income. However, as they become aware that each extra degree of exertion has a smaller probability of resulting to additional output and therefore bonus they will reduce their effort. This also explains why the optimum target will fall as uncertainty increases.

Keren was very careful to add that to some extent the degree of uncertainty rested with the planners themselves. Taking up the issue of supply-induced uncertainty he comments:

> Where there is more than one enterprise, a high target for enterprise i which supplies enterprise j, means a higher degree of uncertainty for enterprise j. Thus a high target may increase production in enterprise i but by increasing uncertainty may reduce production in enterprise j. The longer the chains of supply relationship the more weighty is their element of favouring lower but surer targets. And these chains have grown longer, as the Soviet economy has grown more interdependent.   (On the Tautness of Plans, p.482)

In the early pre-war years of Soviet planning the tendency to underfulfil might have been caused by the planner's ignorance of the production function, and the tastes and beliefs of managers rather than by some optimising behaviour based on the hortatory effects of high targets as Hunter has suggested. Planners did not know how to approximate the target that would have induced maximum effort and more often than not they erred to the side of excess. As time passed and the amount of information over the behaviour of enterprises and the degree of interrelationships within the economy increased, planning became more accurate and therefore underfulfilment was likely to be less common.

In a later extension of his model Keren(5) introduced two goods, rather than just one, and therefore an additional complication in terms of an assortment plan (output mix). As before, the manager maximised a stochastic utility function which included as arguments effort and bonuses subject to the production function of the two goods. Increases in targets increased effort but decreased the probability of fulfilling these targets. Increases in tautness, however, as defined by Keren, did affect negatively the output mix in the sense that it deflected it from the mix desired by the planners. This result allowed Keren to reinterpret Hunter's results in the following manner:

Tautness may increase the value of output but it does so at the cost of worsening the mix. At times when the mix is of little consequence, e.g. when the economy is at a low level of development and is hungry for any commodities it can get, a relatively taut plan may be called for. Where enterprises are relatively undiversified and are limited in their ability to change their assortment of output, the prescription may be similar. Not so when the economy is a highly-developed one and a wrong mix of consumers' goods may pile up as unsaleable inventories, or a wrong mix of producers' goods may lead to production bottlenecks: here a much more conservative plan may be preferable. This is an alternative explanation of Hunter's hypothesis that Soviet planning strategy, which shifted from very ambitious targets in the early days to relatively fulfillable ones later on, was rational in both periods. ('The Incentive Effects ..., p.19)

It is important to note that both Keren and Hunter are attempting to reinterpret and explain the observed behaviour of Soviet planners and enterprises. As the statistical evidence and the discussions presented at the end of this chapter will show, their interpretation is not conflicting with the facts, but it is very hard to prove that it is the only or the correct explanation of the observations. In other words Soviet planners might have been fully aware of the dysfunctional effects of overtaut planning but continued with it because of political pressures or because no one dared to point out that the trade-off had become negative.

4.4   INPUT PLANS AND TAUTNESS

Given the planned level of output, pressure on the enterprise can be increased or decreased by varying the rigidity by which the input plan is enforced. In the extreme case of an enterprise being able to obtain without any restrictions the input required, the pressure that planners could exercise on it via tension in the output or input plan would, ipso facto, disappear. The degree of availability of unplanned (unofficial) inputs was used by Portes in exploring the effects on enterprises of loosely enforced supply plans. It is important at this stage to make explicit the relationship between tautness as is generally understood and the rather special way in which Portes used it:

Tautness essentially characterises the degree of pressure exerted by planners on the enterprise and the economy as a whole, primarily through the plan and associated incentives and the allocation system. The term is often used in a general way to describe various dimensions of the

planners' control over economic units and processes. We
shall be concerned mainly with three particular aspects
of 'tautness': the numerical magnitude of input plans
in relation to other constraints facing the enterprise
and the attainable value of its objective functions;
the degree to which the planners are able to restrict
the possibility of obtaining above-plan inputs; and
the comprehensiveness of central allocation, as measured
by the number of inputs that are centrally allocated.
    ('The Enterprise Under Central Planning', p.197)

The aspects that Portes explores and emphasises is the rigidity of input plans and the capability, or for that matter
willingness, of the Gossnab to police the supply plan and sup-
press the sources of unofficial inputs. In a highly schematic
way the emphasis now moves away from the Keren-Hunter type of

Δ Tension $\rightarrow \Delta$ exertion $\rightarrow \Delta$ output (Δ = changes in)

to

Δ Tension (input plan) $\rightarrow \Delta$ in input utilization

Central planning by means of the physical allocation of
most inputs requires a high degree of complementarity between
them. Planners must attempt to keep the technical coefficients
relating inputs to output relatively constant or at least know
in some detail how these coefficients change as output changes.
The availability of unofficial inputs means that each time
planners changed one of their commands, here the input plan,
the effects of that on the enterprise could be unpredictable.
    Portes assumes that the enterprise is expected to maximize
output Q subject to a minimum profit level and a given set of
inputs. The enterprise is allocated with

x_i i = 1, 2, ... n inputs

which can be purchased at

p_i i = 1, 2, ... n official input prices

There are however

z_i i = 1, 2, ... n

inputs which the enterprise can buy or otherwise obtain outside
the plan. Examples of these inputs will be goods produced by
the enterprise itself for its own use, illegal exchange or sales
of surplus inputs via the operation of 'pushers' (tolkachi) etc.
The cost of these above-plan inputs however, will be higher than
the officially obtained inputs under the plan both because of
their potential illegality and because of the roundabout methods
that the enterprise will have to use in order to obtain them.
    The production function of the enterprise can be written
as $Q = f(y_i + z_i)$, y_i being the inputs that the enterprise can
use constrained however by the x_i plans.   The cost function

93

of these inputs can be written as

$$C_i = (p_i + t_i)z_i + p_i y_i \quad \text{for } i = 1, 2, \ldots n \tag{4.5}$$

The expression $(p_i + t_i)z_i$ indicates that above plan inputs will cost more than the officially allocated ones, i.e. $p_i + t_i$ with t being the extra cost. Portes also makes the assumption that $\partial t_i / \partial z_i > 0$. The problem is then set out as follows:

$$\text{Max. } Q = f(y_i + z_i) \tag{4.6}$$

subject to

(1) $\quad x_i - y_i \geqslant 0 \quad$ the inputs constraint $\tag{4.7}$

(2) $\quad Pf(y_i + z_i) - \sum_{i=1}^{n} \left[p_i y_i + (p_i + t_i)z_i \right] - \Pi^* \geqslant 0 \tag{4.8}$

the profits constraint for $i = 1, 2, \ldots n$, where P is the price at which the output will be sold and Π^* is the minimum planned profit. Maximising with respect to y_i, the necessary conditions can be written as

$$\frac{\partial f}{\partial y_i} (1 + \lambda P) = \lambda P_i + \mu_i \quad \text{for } y_i > 0, \ i = 1 \ldots n$$

This can be written as

$$\frac{\partial y_j}{\partial y_i} = \frac{p_i + \mu_i}{p_j + \mu_j} \quad i \neq j \quad i,j, = 1,2, \ldots n \tag{4.9}$$

where λ stands for the Lagrangean multiplier for the profit constraint and μ_i for the inputs constraint. If the input constraints are not effective, that is the enterprise is using less than the planned amounts at the output maximizing level, then (4.9) becomes $\partial y_j / \partial y_i = p_i / p_j$ which is the standard cost minimising condition. This is not surprising since the enterprise is constrained to make a minimum level of profits. (The rest of the conditions are omitted for the sake of brevity.)

Portes then proceeds to a series of comparative static exercises. He concentrates on the effects of input utilisation when there is an increase in the amount of inputs which the enterprise can purchase at the official prices. The enterprise is assumed to be using at that stage some extra inputs obtained outside the plan and therefore at higher prices than the official ones.

In order to present Portes' case in the most general form it will be assumed that although planners wish enterprises to utilise inputs in fixed ratios, the relative input prices handed down to them need not reflect this. In Figure 4.4 the input

94

FIGURE 4.4   Above-plan input utilisation

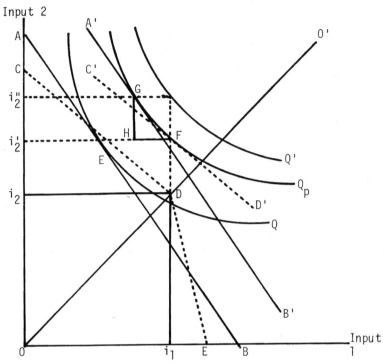

plan consists of allocations of input 1 and 2 equalling Oi_1
and Oi_2. The official relative input prices is given by the
slope of AB and the desired input utilization ratio (norms) by
the slope of OO'. The 'unofficial' above-plan inputs can be
bought at the higher relative prices as indicated by the slopes
of CD (for input 2) and DE for input 1.

An enterprise operating without input plan restrictions
and minimising its costs, would have produced output level Q
utilising the input combination given by E.

The enterprise here however is instructed to produce Q_p
(planned level of output) which it can do only by obtaining an
amount of above-plan input 2 equalling $Oi_2' - Oi_2$ but at the
higher relative input price CD (C'D' being parallel to CD).
The analysis could have been conducted along similar lines if
instead of input 2 the enterprise was obtaining above-plan input 1. The input combination F happens to be cost minimising
but the analysis would still hold even if it was not.

Suppose that input allocation 2 is now increased to Oi_2''.
Strictly speaking the allocation of input 1 should also increase
but since Portes is conducting a comparative static analysis of
very small changes this will have to be disregarded at present.
The effects of the increase in input allocation can now be

separated into two parts. Firstly, a revenue effect (Portes calls this misleadingly an income effect) in the sense that output can now be increased to Q', and secondly, a substitution effect since input 2 can now be bought at the lower official price. The cost minimising enterprise can still produce Q_p using HF less of input 1 and GH more of input 2 (A'B' being parallel to AB). Even if the official input prices did reflect the desired input utilisation norms the increase in input allocation would still produce the substitution effect as long as the enterprise was using above-plan, and therefore, relatively more expensive inputs.

Portes observed that the revenue effect should be generally known to the planners. Irrespective of the relative input prices planners have some idea about the production function of the enterprises and they therefore can guess at the effect on their output of an increase in input allocation. What the planners cannot know however, is the substitution effect which is caused by the availability of extra plan inputs at prices different from the official ones. As long as enterprises have a minimum profits plan to fulfil, then, even if the relative input prices might be meaningless in efficiency terms (i.e. they may not reflect relative scarcities) they will nonetheless affect the decisions of the enterprise. Portes summarised this point thus:

> Income effects will embody the effects of input use of a change provided that these relative prices have remained unchanged for a reasonable period of time the relationship should be well known to the planners. Substitution effects will result from changes in relative prices at the margin which will be unpredictable and a nuisance from the point of view of the planners.
> ('The Enterprise Under Central Planning', p.207)

The nuisance value of the substitution effects arise from the fact that planning presupposes a constancy of the technical co-efficients so that the plans have a chance of being consistent. The greater the availability of inputs outside the plan the greater the scope for input substitution and therefore the less the authority of the plan over the firm's decisions. Portes also proves that completely taut planning in the sense of total absence of above-plan inputs would eliminate any substitution effect and simply force the enterprise to move along a predetermined scale line. Portes does point out however that since the substitution effects depend on the differences in input prices the planners may try to eliminate them by changing the profit plan of the enterprise which is the main motive for the attempts to minimise costs. At this particular point it is worth comparing the conclusions drawn in Chapter 3 of this book (pp.66-7) on the capacity of the enterprise to shift and use inputs amongst the production of different goods but within the input plan. Portes points out that the availability of above-plan inputs may result in unpredictable enterprise behaviour concerning input utilisation when input plans changed thus changing the relative input prices as viewed by the enterprise. In a similar manner the substitutability of inputs within the input plan in the case of the multiproduct enterprise will affect the degree of assortment plan fulfilment.

The logic of Portes' model is, in a mechanistic sense, correct. If the Gossnab has total control over all inputs and enterprises have no discretion over the allocation and use of their supplies, then their reactions to input plan changes would be completely predictable. There is however a counter-intuitive element in the conclusions that as tautness increases the behaviour of the enterprise becomes more predictable. Complete obedience to the instructions of the planners over input utilisation is a meaningless exercise unless it results in output plans being fulfilled or overfulfilled. Although Portes' model does not make any predictions regarding output, it is likely that there would be more rather than less underfulfilment once the input plan was completely and rigidly enforced. For example as was shown on pp.66 of this book the fulfilment of the assortment plan was made easier if the input plan and allocation of inputs was looser. In addition to this some of the evidence reviewed later on suggests that one of the reasons why the incidence and magnitude of output plan underfulfilment fell in the post-war period in the USSR was a relative loosening of control over the supply plan and the possible increase in the availability of above-plan inputs. In other words as control over the input plan became looser the enterprises tended to underfulfil less frequently. This, on its own, does not disprove Portes' contention that the behaviour of the enterprise vis-à-vis input use becomes more predictable as the plan becomes tauter but still leaves open the question of the relevance of his findings over the relationship between planned and actual output.

There is still however a grey area on the analysis of tautness which concerns the fact that Soviet managers tend to exaggerate input requirements precisely because they are acutely aware of the uncertainties surrounding the supplies of inputs. From the point of view of a planner, the taut plan could be seen as a response to the expected hoarding behaviour of enterprises. There is, however, a significant gap in the analysis of tautness at this particular point not only because some of the models outlined, such as Portes', are non-stochastic, but also because the planning of the Soviet enterprises, and in particular inputs allocation, takes place in two stages. Firstly, enterprises receive control figures to which they respond, and then they receive finalised input and output plans. During the first stage of the operations, enterprise managers will be working under uncertainty as they cannot possibly know or guess the demands made upon the supplies by other managers. It is only during the second stage of the operation that the managers will know with some certainty what the inputs allocated to them will be.

Linz and Martin(6) developed a stochastic output maximising model that incorporated an element of supply uncertainty by making explicit the two-stage decision scheme applicable to Soviet enterprises. Their conclusions were that irrespective of the attitude of managers towards risk (lovers, averters, or neutral) the optimal quantity of inputs demanded by them would always be greater than the amount necessary to produce the maximum output subject to a profits constraint. The predictions of this model are interesting insofar as they extend the analysis of a stochastic model of the Soviet enterprise, but they are somewhat weakened by the absence of either a bonus function or the extension of the input demand function over several periods. This is important, because as it will be presently shown, the degree of uncertainty over input supplies, or in general over the operation of the whole central planning process does not remain unchanged over time.

4.5 EMPIRICAL EVIDENCE ON TAUTNESS: A CRITICAL APPRAISAL

This section draws on a number of empirical investigations, simulation exercises and on raw statistical data in an attempt to detect the size, role and importance of tautness in the pre- and post-war planning experience of the Soviet Union. Given that tautness can be observed mostly through the effects on performance rather than as a magnitude in its own right, the evidence is far from conclusive. There are however, a number of pointers that plans did become relatively looser in the post-war period. The trend appeared to continue right up to the tenth FYP (1976-80) although there are some signs that the authorities may attempt to tighten up both on the controls and on the flexibility of action allowed to enterprises during the eleventh FYP.

Excessive plan tautness has been claimed as the root cause of underfulfilment of plans. Tables 4.1 and 4.2 present a summary of the output plan vs actual performance for selected commodities or sectors in the Soviet Union in the pre- and post-war periods. The potential shortcomings of this statistical evidence and also the sources and methods used in deriving the data are set out in a separate note at the end of this chapter. Using the material from these two tables, and subject always to the caveats indicated, two comments are in order.

Firstly of the sixty-nine observations presented in Table 4.1 concerning end of FYPs and seven YP performance only, fifty indicated under-fulfilment, fifteen overfulfilment and four exact or very minor over- or under-fulfilment. In other words more than 70% of the observations concern underfulfilment of plans.

Secondly a comparison of the pre- and post-war performance shows a consistent improvement in the post-war period both in terms of a fall in the incidence and in the magnitude of the underfulfilment. This is confirmed by the data in Table 4.2. A

TABLE 4.1   Percentage under (−) or over (+) fulfilment of plan at the end of planning periods

Product(s)	1 End of 1st FYP 1932-3	2 End of 2nd FYP 1937	3 End of 4th FYP 1950	4 End of 5th FYP 1955	5 End of 7 year plan 1965	6 End of 8th FYP 1970	7 End of year 1966	8 End of year 1967
Coal	−14.2	−16.0	+4.4	−4.4	−4.6	−6.8	−65.7	+15.3
Steel	−43.2	+4.1	−7.4	−2.4	+2.8	−8.3	−4.7	
Pig iron	−38.0	−9.3	−1.5	−1.4	−1.9	−10.0		
Electrical power	−39.0	−4.7	+11.2	+3.6	−0.5	−12.4	−29.2	−17.5
Rolled metal		*				−5.1	+27.2	+34.6
Oil	−2.7	−39.0	+7.0	+1.4	+3.3	*	+4.6	+13.9
Gas		+13.7			−13.8	+13.7	−15.0	−2.9
Machine tools						−6.6		
Motor vehicles					−5.1	−36.1		
Cement		−28.5	−2.8	*	−7.1	−7.1		
Fertilisers		−64.4			−9.7	−12.7	+15.0	+44.5
Tractors			+116.0	+7.4		−25.0	−5.0	
Chemical fibres					−38.8	−22.6		+19.5
Plastics						−24.0		−22.2
Leather footwear	−65.4	+1.6	−15.0	−13.9	−5.6	+20.5	+51.0	
Cotton fabrics		−32.3	−16.7	−5.9	*			
Wool fabrics		−52.2	−2.4	+5.5				
Sugar		−3.1	−4.1	−22.7	−75.0			

For sources and commentary see notes at the end of chapter.

* denotes an almost 100% fulfilment.

TABLE 4.2   Percentage of plans fulfilled of industrial products

	NUMBER OF PRODUCTS			
	Second FYP (1933-37)		Seven YP (1959-65)	
	Producer	Consumer	Producer	Consumer
130 and over	1	1	1	-
110 - 129.9	3	3	-	3
102 - 109.9	2	3	5	2
99 - 101.9	4	1	2	-
95 - 98.9	2 ⎫	2 ⎫	5 ⎫	1 ⎫
90 - 94.9	3 ⎪	2 ⎪	3 ⎪	4 ⎪
80 - 89.9	8 ⎬ 80%	7 ⎬ 78%	6 ⎬ 75%	1 ⎬ 64%
60 - 79.9	10 ⎪	6 ⎪	6 ⎪	3 ⎪
Less than 49 - 59.9	19 ⎭	13 ⎭	4 ⎭	- ⎭
Total number of products	52	38	32	14
Median percentage of fulfilment	72.2	77.8	88.9	93.7

NB   The figures in the long brackets express the number of products whose plans were underfulfilled as percentage of the total sample for that group.

For sources and commentary see note at the end of chapter.

summarised verions of Table 4.1 is presented in Table 4.3.
     It is interesting to observe the discrepancies between the end of year performance in 1966 and 1967 and the overall outcome of the eighth FYP. The discrepancies could be explained away by the simple expedient of assuming that the plan was changed to ensure a reasonable or acceptable underfulfilment. This particular point will be examined in some detail further on.
     Some additional evidence presented in Table 4.4 on the actual vs planned performance for a series of industrial ministries in the post-war period was collected by Granick(7).   Although the decision-making unit was not the enterprise but the ministry the results did reflect the continuing loosening of the plans in the post-war period. Granick points out that the improvement in ministerial performance during 1969-77 as far as sales

TABLE 4.3   Incidence and magnitude of underfulfilment
(FYPs and SYP only)

	Less than or equal to 10%		More than 10%	
	No. of goods or industries	% of total	No. of goods or industries	% of total
Pre-war	4	27	11	73
Post-war	22	63	13	37

Source: Table 4.1

The percentage of total refers to the number of observations of underfulfilment for each period.

TABLE 4.4   Data on the performance of output plans (1949-56)
and sales plan (1969-77) of a sample of industrial
ministries

Period 1949-56	Period 1969-77
Data from 17-23 ministries for 7 years and for 10 ministries during 1953 only.	Data from 21-23 ministries for each year.
During this period at least one ministry under-fulfilled its plans in all but one year (1949).	In two years, 1969 and 1972, 29% of the ministries in the sample missed their target. But in the remaining 7 years there was only one ministerial underfulfilment out of 157 ministerial observations (i.e. 22 ministries approx. × 7 years = 154).

Source: Granick, The Ministry as the maximising unit, p.262.

NB The source does not give details as to the degree of underfulfilment but the sample excluded ministries processing
foodstuffs as their performance was linked to the erratic
performance of the agricultural sector.

are concerned does not give any indication as to the actual
achievement of rates of profits. The latter was becoming by
then as important a planned index as the level of sales.   In
other words the improved actual vs planned sales might not be
an indicator of looser planning if taken in conjunction with a
tighter profits plan. As there was no evidence on the actual
performance of rates profits of ministries this proposition
remains purely conjectural.

Some additional evidence on the actual vs planned behaviour
was provided by a simulation exercise undertaken by Dolan[8].
The aim here was to generate conditions under which plans were
likely to be underfulfilled and observe Hunter-type performance
curves of the economy as these conditions changed.   The frame
of reference of this model was the change in the degree of
planned pressure between the first and second five year plans
in the Soviet Union. The usefulness of this simulation lies in
that it provides some a priori rationale and explanation of the
observed changes in performance.

Tautness in the plans was introduced by allowing for bottlenecks to appear, by capacity limitations and decreasing re-
turns to scale. Different bonus functions introduced the
ratchet effect of overfulfilment and also varied the financial
rewards of producing exactly to plan.

The simulated actual versus the planned performance of the
economy as illustrated by the Hunter-type curves were very interesting. For bonus functions which encouraged exact fulfilment the curve looked like that labelled A in Figure 4.5.   The
curve would not of course coincide with the 45° line because
the bonus scheme was not the only influence on the achieved output. Schemes which reduced the ratchet effect of overfulfilment
resulted in curves like B, i.e. they encouraged overfulfilment.
For models of the economy using an input-output matrix with zero
or near zero elements above the diagonal (i.e. very little or
no inter-dependence amongst the various sectors) Dolan obtained
curves like C, whereas as the degree of inter-dependence grew the
curves became more like D. The more interdependent the economy
became the greater the seriousness of underfulfilling the plan
in terms of the difference between the actual and the planned
magnitudes.

Dolan used these simulation results to explain the behaviour of planners in the formulation of the first and second five
year plans in the Soviet Union. Over time there was a reduction
in the degree of tautness in the plans. This can be interpreted
in a number of ways.

For a start planners realised that they had over-extended the
capacity limits of the economy. Perhaps they had thought that
the economy's performance was more like that of curve E in
Figure 4.6 whereas it was more like that of F.   The outcome of
this over-estimation could have been made worse by a developing
credibility gap and cynicism in the lower planning echelons plus
an exhaustion of X-efficiency reserves. The latter concept was

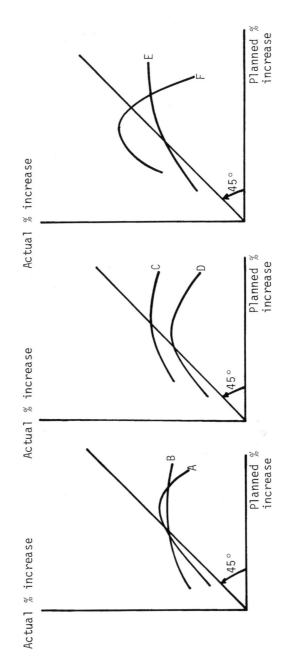

FIGURE 4.5   A simulation exercise on tautness

developed by Leibenstein(9) in at attempt to measure welfare losses caused not so much by allocative inefficiencies (monopolies, monopsonies etc.) but by reasons internal to the production unit).

X-inefficiency exists if there is a difference between the maximum output that can be achieved over the actual output. It is important to stress that the reallocation of resources that would eliminate X-inefficiency (i.e. generate gains by tapping X-efficiency reserves) refers to internal reallocation rather than shifts of resources and inputs from sector to sector. The causes of X-inefficiency as specified by Leibenstern although they pertain to a market economy, are particularly relevant to the case of the Soviet enterprise:

> I suggest four reasons for X-inefficiency connected with the basic notion of variable performance for given units of the inputs: contracts for labor are incomplete; the production function is not completely specified or known; not all inputs are marketed or, if marketed, are not available on equal terms to all buyers; and the effective utilization of an input depends on the degree of motivational pressure, as well as on other motivational factors. The responses to such pressures, whether in the nature of effort, search, or the utilization of new information, may be a significant part of residual economic growth ...

> (Beyond Economic Man, p.46)

These particular sources of X-inefficiency could be easily detected in the context of a Soviet enterprise and they may also serve to illustrate the point why additional pressure, i.e. tautness, may eliminate X-inefficiency at the start but possibly end up generating it if pressure is carried to extremes.

Finally, as the degree of interdependence in the economy grew it became obvious that the curves were shifting downwards and to the left, thus increasing the potential losses of output generated by tauter plans. This led to an easing of the pressure.

The evidence produced so far appears to confirm the casual empiricism of Hunter and Keren, neither of whom backed up their interpretations with specific rather than anecdotal data. The incidence and magnitude of underfulfilment declined in the post-war period compared to pre-war and the decline was sustained with minor variations till the late 1970s.

Whether the reduction in tautness was the outcome of growing uncertainty over the input-output links in the economy or a deliberate shift of emphasis by the planners towards optimising the relationship between the beneficial and dysfunctional aspects of taut plans, remains debatable. As will be shown presently the evidence is subject to alternative interpretations. It is certain however that tautness is not caused by purely random errors, i.e. it is non-deliberate and unplanned. The reduction

in the incidence and magnitude of underfulfilment indicates
that if planners made genuine errors they learnt by them and
corrected them over time. The random error approach would be
valid only if the incidence and size of underfulfilment and
overfulfilment remained unchanged over time, and clearly it did
not.

The points that have been raised so far can now be summarised and the concepts of tautness reappraised in the light of
the empirical evidence presented.

Firstly, one of the reasons plans are not fulfilled is the
imperfections of the supply system.   Improvements in the
operations of Gossnab will improve the chances of fulfilment.
In other words, input of exertion and inputs of physical goods
(or economies in their use) are not the same thing.   Portes'
special interpretation of tautness in terms of the rigidity of
enforcement of the inputs plan make no predictions regarding the
degree of fulfilment of output plans. The model was after all,
designed to explore one of the many aspects of tautness.   The
developments in the supply side of planning which were examined
in Chapter 3 of this book do point however to a relative loosening of control over the number of centrally distributed inputs.
The greater involvement of ministerial glavki, direct links between enterprises, the gradual introduction of khozraschet into
Gossnab might mean greater opportunities for illegal trading,
exchanges and manipulation of accounts over the naryad-zakaz
etc.   Table 2.2, p.36, in Chapter 3 provided some direct evidence that in the period 1965-73 the ministries as opposed to
the Gossnab itself or its organs became more important in terms
of the number of goods whose distribution they planned.   The
number of goods distributed by the Gossnab and its organs fell
from 18,530 in 1965 to 12,529 in 1968 and to 12,018 in 1973, a
fall of more than 35% within nine years. So although the centralised allocation and the certificates system remains, as the
administration becomes decentralised the greater the ease by
which it might be abused and manipulated. Whether these trends
will be reversed remains to be seen.   Furthermore, Tables 2.5
and 2.6 on pp.44 and 45 of this book show that the percentage of
inventories held by consumer enterprises is quite high compared
to that of the Gossnab. As long as inventories of goods are in
the hands of producers or consumers and not of Gossnab and its
organs, the greater the ease by which unplanned input trans-
actions can be undertaken. A weaker enforcement of the input
plan allows greater degree of freedom in fulfilling both the
assortment plan and the overall output. The growing complexity
and interdependence of the economy may have resulted in less
rigid enforcement of the supply plans, and as a consequence, to
an improvement of the actual performance of the enterprise.
This last point is, of course, speculatory as there is no direct
quantitative evidence linking the degree of tautness of the input plans and actual performance. By the nature of the game it
would be impossible, anyway, to obtain information concerning

the comparative performance of enterprises with and without access to unplanned or 'illegal' inputs.

Secondly, it is likely that the postulated growth of information about the economy led to a fall rather than an increase in uncertainty and hence planners could approximate with greater accuracy the true productive capacity of enterprises. In other words the effect of uncertainty might have worked the other way around. The targets became more realistic and performance improved because the level of uncertainty decreased.

Thirdly, the changes in the bonus system since 1965 might have contributed to the ease of tension. Wiles' contention that bonus schemes may cause tension raises a number of issues.

The bonus scheme that encourages overfulfilment might have been the result of planner's tension rather than the cause of it. Planners knew that there was excess capacity reserves and hence used taut plans to extract additional output. The dysfunctional effects of a purely hortatory (moral-psychological) approach were likely to set in very quickly. Hence the need to reinforce plans with financial incentives.

The changes in the bonus schemes since 1965 point to the increasing discomfort by which Soviet planners viewed overfulfilment. The incentive schemes introduced with the 1965 reforms discouraged overfulfilment and the post-1972 schemes went to great lengths to ensure that the overfulfilment of plans in general and of counter-plans in particular was penalised. Enterprises are now encouraged to put forward counter-plans and are rewarded for their exact fulfilment. One would expect that the self-imposed degree of tautness would lead to a smaller dispersion of over and underfulfilment of plans. In a sense bonuses are substitutes for tension, subject however to the restriction that the basic plan must be fulfilled if bonuses are to be received at all. All these points are discussed in detail in Chapter 6 of this book. There are at present no disaggregate data available to test the proposition that looser plans were caused by changes in the bonus schemes. It is however counter-intuitive to assume that planners first introduced an incentive scheme which causes tautness and then proceeded to loosen the plans whilst changing the bonus system at the same time. The logical sequence would appear to be: taut planning reinforced by bonus schemes which encourage overfulfilment. Any changes in tautness caused by economic or political considerations are then reflected on to the changes in the incentive scheme as well.

Managers are assumed to be bonus maximisers or at least bonuses are an important percentage of their salary. Whether changes in plans or bonus schemes affect performance is an empirical question which is explored at length in Chapters 5 and 6.

Fourthly, the analysis of both Keren and Hunter contained the idea that there is an optimum degree of tautness towards which planners are moving either through trial and error (Hunter) or through a bonus system that rewards effort (Keren). This

concept of optimality is purely spurious and ultimately meaningless when looked at from a macro rather than a micro point of
view, especially if planners are interested in the optimisation
of a (non) linear programming sense of either sectors or the
whole of the economy. Zauberman makes this point quoting from
a study by Vainshtein:

> ... who showed that overfulfilment of targets does indeed
> undermine the equilibrium at optimum unless special cor-
> rections are introduced to preserve the structural char-
> acteristics of output, by raising inputs of non-producible
> factors, say labour, or their productivity in some sectors
> assuming that better returns would not be obtained in
> other sectors. The rationale of the overfulfilment rule
> can just as well be seen in the more or less conscious
> understanding that efficient solutions of the plan
> problem is beyond the possibilities of the traditional
> planning techniques.(10)

The fact that this particular study referred specifically to
overfulfilment does not invalidate its conclusions because
the same could have been said for underfulfilment. Optimum
tautness by definition must imply a degree of under or overfulfilment of plans since actual and planned will coincide only
in a world of perfect knowledge - i.e. an assumption of perfect
certainty.

The near-obsession of western observers of the Soviet economy with optimum tautness has found little or no response with
their Soviet counterparts. Indeed the concept does not even
appear in the surveyed Soviet literature which concentrates
instead on an operational definition of 'napryazhenost'
(tautness) that can be incorporated in bonus schemes. Two
examples will suffice to illustrate the way in which Soviet
economists define tautness.

A straightforward definition of tautness would incorporate
the degree of utilisation of equipment as of industrial capacity.
Egiazaryan proposed the following formula(11):

$$T = \left(\frac{a_1}{a_0} A_1 + \frac{a_1}{a_n} A_2 \right) \qquad (4.10)$$

where T stands for the degree of tautness, a_1 is the planned
level of output, a_0 is the base year on which the index is
based, a_n is the normative level of the index, and A_1 and A_2
are the 'dynamic' and 'static' weights respectively. The coefficient a_n can be thought as the 'normal' level of utilisation
of capacity - if the indexes referred to industrial output. It
then follows that a_1/a_0 is the percentage increase over the base
year and a_1/a_n is the percentage increase over the normative
level of that index. The T index can then be incorporated in

a bonus formula once the A_1 and A_2 weights have been decided by the planner. Since however the a_1/a_0 ratio attaches the same importance to, say, a 10% increase in the plan whether it starts from a 50% or a 99% utilisation of capacity the formula is modified to a non linear form:

$$T = \frac{a_0}{a_n} \left(\frac{a_1}{a_0}\right)^2 \tag{4.11}$$

so that the percentage increase over the base year is now given an additional weight but the degree of tautness is proportionately dependent on the existing average level of the index in relation to its norm. In terms of a formula of industrial capacity utilisation a_0/a_n would stand for the average level of excess capacity at the beginning of the plan period. The ratio a_1/a_0 is squared in order to emphasise the importance of the growth of the indexes over time. The formulas as presented in (4.10) or (4.11) can be quickly transformed into an operational rule because the only 'subjective' elements in it are the A_1 and A_2 coefficients, and possibly the a_n coefficient unless defined on the basis of some average.

An interesting stochastic measurement of tautness is presented by Volkov(12). The definition of tautness is simply

$$T^* = \frac{P}{P^*} \tag{4.12}$$

where T^* is the measure of tautness, P is the planned target and P^* is the probability of that target being fulfilled. So if the plan envisaged 100 units of output with P^* at 50% then the tautness index would stand at 200 units, indicating that it would take a notional (or nominal plan) of 200 to achieve the actual planned target of 100. Volkov's formula directs attention to the stochastic aspects of tautness without however explaining why or how it arises. For a given P as T^* increases the level of uncertainty P^* would increase as the probability of fulfilling the plan fell. To the extent however that planned targets are not fixed i.e. they are subject to revision then both the hortatory effect and the degree of uncertainty that tautness induces must be variable.

Finally, the discussion on tautness must allow for a particularly awkward characteristic of Soviet planning, that is the continuous change in plans. The notion of a fixed plan exerting constant and continuous pressure on the enterprise is just not true. Although anecdotal evidence in this area abounds, there are very few data available on the effects of changes in plan on fulfilment. The evidence however such as it is, is crucial in quantifying the importance of the plan and of plan discipline on the behaviour of the enterprise.

Granick quoted the results of a study on the performance of two groups of about 100 Soviet industrial enterprises whose

Plan Tautness and Enterprise Behaviour

plans were changed. Comparisons were made between the amount
of actual sales of each enterprise during 1970 and both the enterprise's original sales plan for the year and the final sales
plan. The results are presented in Table 4.5.

TABLE 4.5   Fulfilment of annual sales plan for 1970   (%)

Plan Fulfilment	Group 1		Group 2	
	Original	Final	Original	Final
Average percentage for the group	102.2	102.8	102.5	103.5
(Standard deviation)	(2.68)	(2.29)	(7.45)	(3.69)
Enterprises not fulfilling plan	17.7	2.4	33.1	5.6
Enterprises fulfilling 106% or more	7.1	9.4	22.6	14.5

Source: Granick, The Ministry as a maximizing unit, p.260

        If tautness was the reason why enterprises were not likely
to fulfil their sales plan in 1970, then the change in plan reduced the incidence of underfulfilment quite dramatically by 86%
in Group 1 and 83% in Group 2. At the same time the change in
plans increased the incidence of overfulfilment by 32% in Group
1 but reduced by 36% in Group 2.   In this case the changes
were not as dramatic as that of the fall in the incidence of
underfulfilment. Admittedly there is nothing in the evidence
to suggest that plans for individual enterprises were scaled
down because the originals were unduly optimistic.   Breakdowns
in the supply side could have been just as valid an explanation.
What is interesting here however is the fact that irrespective
of the causes of the change in plans, the changes led to a decrease in the incidence of both under and, in one case, overfulfilment of the plan.
        A much more detailed study of the relationship between or-
iginal and final plans and plan changes in general was undertaken by Khaikin(13). Using data from 154-210 industrial enterprises and associations in the Ukraine over the 1970-78 period,
he examined the degrees of fulfilment of the original and revised annual sales plans of these enterprises. His findings in
that area can be summarised in four steps.
        Firstly, the performance of the enterprises over the time
period can be tabulated thus:

109

Plan Tautness and Enterprise Behaviour

Initial Plan	Final Revised Plan
68.3% fulfilled it	94.4% fulfilled it
31.7% did not	5.6% did not

Given that one-third of the sample of the enterprise did not
fulfil their initial plan but almost 95% of them fulfilled the
final version, then it must follow that the revision would have
been downwards.

Secondly, of the 31.7% of the enterprises that did not
fulfil their initial plan, 7.3% (of the 31.7%) had their plans
left unchanged and 92.7% (of the 31.7%) had their plans revised.
Needless to say the revision in practically all these cases
(98% to be precise) was downwards.

Thirdly, of the 68.3% of the enterprise that did fulfil
their initial plan about half of them had their plans changed.
Three-quarters of these revisions were upwards.

Finally, Khaikin submitted his data to a battery of statistical tests. Enterprises were separated into groups depending on whether they had fulfilled or not the initial and final
plans. This generated four classes of enterprises, i.e. those
that underfulfilled the original but overfulfilled the final
plan and so on. A number of regression equations were then run
using the following simple model:

$$\text{\% fulfilment of final plan} = A + B(\text{\% fulfilment of original plan})$$

With a few exceptions the results were poor thus indicating
that there was no apparent systematic relationship between revisions of plans and the original level of fulfilment. This was
not surprising in view of the fact that planners did try to ensure that the plan revisions yielded an eventual fulfilment of
the plan but at the same time avoided too much overfulfilment.

Data on the original and revised plans and the performance
of the enterprise were then tabulated yielding some highly interesting results on potential frequencies of revisions and degree of fulfilment. Khaikin summarised his findings thus:

... any enterprise not fulfilling its original target
has at least two chances out of three of getting the
plan reduced, and the chances may rise to nine out of
ten or more for an enterprise which fulfils its original
plan by more than 90% ... But as the degree of overfulfilment of the original plan rises the chances that
it will be unchanged or reduced decline sharply and the
chances that it will be raised predominates. In fact
when the plan is overfulfilled by 5% there are already
three chances out of four that it will be raised and
for over 13% overfulfilment an increase occurs in every
case ...

> The overall level of plan discipline has been low.
> Target revisions have predominantly been aimed at
> eliminating inaccuracies in the original plans. This
> has reduced enterprises' incentives to reveal reserves
> in order to fulfil or overfulfil their original plans,
> in view of the very high probability that they would
> be revised either downward if the targets were not ful-
> filled or upwards if they were overfulfilled ...
> (An Analysis of the State of Plan Discipline ... pp.70-71)

Khaikin obtained similar results when he used the plans
for labour productivity, wages and average wage per worker.

The Granick and Khaikin studies taken together provide val-
uable and much-needed hard evidence that plan revisions do occur
and that planners try to ensure that underfulfilment is minimised. This empirical evidence taken on its own does not necessarily disprove that tautness exists, because the problem of
why enterprises underfulful their original plan still remains.
The evidence however does raise a number of issues concerning
the ratchet effect in planning (i.e. basing plans in period on
the actual performance in period t-1) when taken in conjunction
with the bonus scheme. These points will be examined in greater
detail in the next chapter.

It is also important to note that changes in plan discussed
by Granick referred to those of enterprises rather than ministries. This particular point was used by Granick to raise a
possibly fundamental objection to using the enterprise as the
basic microeconomic unit in analysing the behaviour of the
Soviet planning process. Granick suggests that the ministry
should be used instead. The reasons offered were two-fold.
Firstly, the frequency of changes in enterprise plans made the
enterprises an unsuitable unit of organisation for observing the
influence of plan on behaviour, especially as most of the changes
were designed to aid those enterprises that were not fulfilling
their plans. Secondly, the introduction of five-year control
figures in the ninth FYP (1971-75) apparently shifted the burden
and the penalties in terms of lost bonuses, for underfulfilment
to ministries rather than enterprises.

There are a number of observations that can be made on
these points. For a start, there is no hard evidence that the
overall plans for ministries in the Soviet Union do not also
change. Indeed, there is some evidence at least for other
planned economies that plans for ministries do change(14).
There is no apparent reason to believe that the Soviet Union is
an exception. Furthermore, it is an inescapable conclusion
that the performance of the ministry reflects the sum total of
the performance of the subordinate enterprises. Concentrating
on the behaviour of ministries will simply cast a veil over the
lower, and therefore even more basic units of the Soviet economy,
thus eliminating them from scientific investigation. Finally,
it is precisely the instability of the plan handed down to the

111

enterprise that makes the analysis of its behaviour all the more interesting and challenging. In a world of absolute certainty and completely unchanging plans there would be nothing to observe or investigate except a totally predictable 100% plan fulfilment.

4.6 CONCLUSIONS

Of all the causes of tautness outlined in this chapter the least convincing one is the claim that planners pursue an optimising relationship between the extra output generated by taut plans and the degree of underfulfilment. A more reasonable explanation of the causes and variations in the degrees of tautness can be developed along the following lines. Planners exert pressure because they know that there is excess capacity and hidden resources. The purely hortatory effect will dissipate quickly; hence the need to reinforce taut plans with bonus schemes that encourage exertion. The imperfections of the supply system and the growth of interdependence in the economy will make the use of deliberate taut plans an expensive way of extracting output at the margin. Errors can cause, occasionally, tautness but they cannot explain the reasons why tautness as measured by plan performance decreased over time.

Plan revisions may, on the surface, appear to reduce the tension, however caused, but still do not explain or resolve the problem why enterprises tend to under(over)fulfil their initial plans. Plan changes however might make nonsense of the claim that planned tautness is a way to extract additional output if, as the evidence suggests, most of the plan changes aid enterprises that are likely to underfulfil. If enterprises come to expect that they will be rescued, then a taut plan might not be resisted and, of course, no serious attempt will be made to fulfil it. The evidence on this point, however, is scattered far from conclusive.

The bonus scheme can now be seen as one way by which planners can encourage the enterprise to produce more output and also more information about capacity. Here the plan per se is not what induces a reduction in X-inefficiency; this is achieved by the pecuniary rewards of the incentive scheme.

In the post-1965 period planners put greater reliance on bonus schemes and stable targets in encouraging enterprisers to put forward higher plans. In the 1970s the emphasis changed even further towards exact fulfilment of plans. The following two chapters will explore in greater detail both the theory of and evidence on incentive schemes and their influence on the behaviour of the Soviet enterprise.

Plan Tautness and Enterprise Behaviour

Notes on Tables 4.1 and 4.2

Sources:

Table 4.1   The first five columns were derived from A. Nove's
An Economic History of the USSR, Pelican Books, London 1972,
pp.191,225,291,340 and 353.   All the data were expressed in
physical terms i.e. tons, thousands units, metres, etc.   The
degrees of fulfilment was derived by taking actual performance
at the end of period minus the plan divided by the planner performance.   Column six was derived from a paper presented at the
1971 conference of the National Association for Soviet and East
European Studies by A. Nove and R. Clarke entitled The Soviet
Five-Year Plan.   Again all the data were in physical units.
Finally, columns seven and eight were derived from P.J.D. Wiles
(Ed.) The Predictions of Communist Economic Performance, Cambridge University Press, Cambridge 1971, pp.288-89 and 305. The
unit of measurement here was percentage annual growth rates.

Table 4.2 was derived from V.G. Treml and R. Farrell (Eds.), The
Development of the Soviet Economy: Plan and Performance, F.
Praeger, New York 1968, p.66.   The source did not give a detailed classification of the goods involved so there is no way
of making Tables 4.1 and 4.2 comparable.   Neither did it indicate the units of measurement. This is important given the
problem of measuring the plan performance in value terms over
long periods of time.
    In order to give a degree of consistency and comparabili-
ties for the pre- and post-war periods in Table 4.1 the selection
of products or industries was limited mostly to those areas
where data were available for periods examined.   But even so
there are discrepancies as the definitions and groupings of
products changed over time (especially in the case of fertili-
sers which may include either mineral or chemical types).
    Plans did change during the plan period, hence both the
degree of under or overfulfilment could be changed or modified.
There were insufficient data to allow consistent comparisons
between, say, original plan version, modified version and actual
outcome. In other words, planners could modify continuously and
almost certainly did, the degree of plan pressure.   It is also
important to note that the very wide groupings of goods hide a
multitude of sins (or virtues) concerning the performance of
individual enterprises as opposed to industries or sectors.

Notes

1. H. Hunter, 'Optimal Tautness in Development Planning', in Economic Development and Cultural Change, Vol.9, July 1961, pp.561-572.

2. M. Keren, 'On the Tautness of Plans', Review of Economic Studies, Vol.39, October 1972, pp.469-486.

3. R.D. Portes, 'The Enterprise Under Central Planning', Review of Economic Studies, Vol.36, April 1969, pp.197-212.

4. P.J.D. Wiles, The Political Economy of Communism, Basil Blackwell, Oxford 1964, p.261.

5. M. Keren, 'The Incentive Effects of Plan Targets and Priorities in a Disaggregate Model', Journal of Comparative Economics, Vol.3, No.1, March 1979, pp.1-26.

6. S.J. Linz and R.E. Martin, 'Soviet Enterprise Behaviour Under Uncertainty', Journal of Comparative Economics, Vol.6, No.1, March 1982, pp.24-36.

7. D. Granick, 'The Ministry as the Maximizing Unit in Soviet Industry', Journal of Comparative Economics, Vol.4, Sept. 1980, pp.255-273, esp. p.260 and pp.261-63.

8. E. Dolan, The Teleological Period in Soviet Economic Planning, Yale Economic Essays, Spring 1970, pp.3-41.

9. H. Leibenstein, Beyond Economic Man: A new foundation for microeconomics, Harvard University Press, Massachusetts 1976, Ch.3.

10. A. Zauberman, 'Planning Models' in H.H. Hohman, M. Kaser and K. Thalheim (Eds.). The New Economic Systems in Eastern Europe, C. Hunt & Co., London 1975, p.382.

11. G.A. Egiazaryan, Material'noe stimulirovanie rosta effectivnost' promyshlennogo proizvodstve, Moscow 1976, pp.167-82.

12. L.I. Volkov, Opredelenie razmera fondov material'nogo pooshchreniya khozraschetnya podrazdelenii predpriyatiya, in Yu. G. Smirnov (Ed.), Ekonomiko-matematicheskie modeli i metody v organizatsii i planirovanii na predpriyatiyakh, Moscow 1975, pp.18-27.

13. V.P. Khaikin, 'An Analysis of the State of Plan Discipline in Enterprises' Matekon, Winter 1981-82, pp.53-74. Translation of article that appeared in Ekonomika i Matematicheskie Metody Vol.16, No.15, 1981, pp.930-943. All references to this article are from the Matekon translation.

14. M. Keren, 'The Ministry, Plan Changes and Ratchet in Planning', Journal of Comparative Economics Vol.6, No.4, Dec. 1982, pp.327-342. Keren used data for a number of industrial ministries in GDR to show that the plans of these ministries were subject to changes as well as those of their subordinate enterprise.

Chapter Five

BONUS SYSTEMS AND ENTERPRISE BEHAVIOUR

5.1 INTRODUCTION

Chapter 3 on the neoclassical models of the Soviet enterprise
showed that only a very limited amount of useful information or
predictions could be derived from them.   A potentially more
fruitful approach is to explore the implications of different
bonus systems within a framework of taut planning.   In other
words combine some of the elements of Chapter 4 with a more
sophisticated set of stochastic models of bonus and managerial
utility functions. The aim here will be to explore the problems
facing both the planners and the managers in designing and res-
ponding to a system of financial rewards that will encourage the
fulfilment of taut but realistic plans.   The point raised by
Wiles(1), that the neoclassical theory of the firm is essentially
a theory of markets, comes out in sharp relief but in an opposite way, when examining the theory of the Soviet enterprise
which does not involve market interactions. Here the interaction
is between the planners and the planned. Taking the relatively
easy approach of a bonus maximising objective function disregards however all the problems involved both with the ratchet
effect of plan and the degree of effort (and its attendant disutility) of operating within a taut plan.   The role of the
Gossnab in this particular context is now subsumed within the
tautness of the inputs plan vis-à-vis the planned output and the
rest of the targets. Hence a combined bonus-tautness approach
is likely to offer a more varied view of enterprise behaviour
patterns.   It is important however to emphasise that the
models presented are not meant to be a generalised view of the
operations of the Soviet enterprise, but just another way of exploring its behaviour and, hopefully, producing some testable
predictions.
     This chapter surveys various bonus schemes developed by
both Soviet and western authors.   As this has become something
of a growth area for research, especially in the west, the survey had to be by necessity very selective in two senses:
     Firstly, the aim is to present schemes of increasing order

Bonus Systems and Enterprise Behaviour

of complexity building towards the actual Soviet practice in the late 1970s. This is not a purely academic exercise because the outlines of the various suggestions allows the pin-pointing of both empirically testable propositions and a clarification of the issues underlying the Soviet reforms of the incentives in 1965 and 1972. Secondly, Soviet and western analytical work of a purely normative nature (i.e. suggestions for reform, variations of the existing schemes etc.) has been omitted in favour of building up a theoretical and empirical picture of the Soviet system as it actually is and operates.

5.2 BONUS SYSTEMS AND MODELS

As Chapter 4 indicated, the bonus scheme is an important instrument used by planners in reinforcing and bolstering the hortatory effects, if any, of taut planning. The side effects however of incentive schemes that encourage overfulfilment are well known:

Firstly, they encourage rather than discourage the concealment of productive capacity from the planners as this enables the enterprise to overfulfil. Secondly, they generate the ratchet effect since every overfulfilment, or even exact fufilment of a plan, will imply that next period will start from the 'achieved level'. It could be argued that the principle of taut planning from the achieved level is a separate issue from that of the design of incentive schemes. This however would detract not only from the actual Soviet planning techniques but also from the fact that this practice is an extension of taut planning and hence an integral part of the problems surrounding bonus functions. A key problem therefore in designing bonus schemes is the avoidance of the ratchet effect. In purely analytical terms this means that the bonus system must incorporate some intertemporal element, i.e. maximisation of bonuses over time and at the same time allow for uncertainty.

Weitzman(2) summarised these points under a static and a dynamic problem:

> There are two basic incentive problems associated with a standard reward system: one is static and the other is dynamic. The immediate difficulty is essentialy a static problem of misrepresentation which has to do with bluffing or gaming in hopes of influencing the plan while it is being formulated. The worker or manager will typically try to convince his superior that (performance indicator such as output) y is likely to be small, thereby entitling him to a lower (target) q and a bonus that is easier to attain ... The dynamic incentive problem arises from the well-known tendency of planners to use current performance as a criterion in determining future goals. This tendency has sometimes been called the 'ratchet principle' of

116

economic planning because current performance acts like a notched gear wheel in fixing the point of departure for next period's target ... In such situations agents face a dynamic trade-off between present rewards from better current performance and future losses from the assignment of higher targets.

As the survey of the incentive system unfolds it will become apparent that there is no easy simultaneous solution - if any at all - to this twin static-dynamic problem.

A minimum requirement for a simple bonus scheme would be to devise a function that would reward fulfilment but penalise deviations from the plan. For example setting bonus B to

$$B = AQ - C(Q - Q_p)^\alpha \qquad (5.1)$$

where A, C and α given positive parameters and Q and Q_p standing from now on as the actual and planned levels of output or any other target. The planners would penalise here both over and underfulfilment by the simple expedient of setting α to even integers such as 2, 4, 6 etc.(3)   Irrespective however of the actual numerical values of A and C and as long as $\alpha > 1$ it is easy to show that a bonus function such as (5.1) may have undesirable side-effects. For example the level of actual output Q that will maximise B in (5.1) will always be greater than Q_p. Maximising B with respect to Q and rearranging

$$(Q - Q_p)^{\alpha-1} = \frac{A}{\alpha C} \qquad (5.2)$$

Since $A/\alpha C > 0$ by definition, then $Q > Q_p$ and the enterprises will tend to overfulfil their plans over time.   This formula does assume that managers are bonus maximisers, but even more importantly, it assumes that they will disregard the fact that consistent overfulfilment will lead to higher plans in successive time periods. The analysis can now be made more realistic by exploring the properties of an incentive system that allows explicitly for the disincentive effect of the ratchet i.e. the practice of planning from the achieved level.

Gindin(4) developed such a model by using a managerial utility defined as

$$U = f(B, T_n, T_o) \qquad (5.3)$$

The function contained three arguments.   Firstly the bonus B receivable on fulfilling the plan. The bonus function itself was defined as

$$B = g(T_o, Q) \qquad (5.4)$$

with T_o being the current plan or target and Q the actual achieved level of target. From here on both T and Q are assumed to be

117

output.   Secondly, the current target level of output, T_0, which is given, and finally the new target T_n, i.e. the plan for next period. To simplify the analysis it was assumed that utility was to be measured in the same units as bonus and that it varied at the same rate as bonuses did. The current plan T_0 will affect utility via the bonus function because bonuses will be received only when actual output Q equals T_0.
   The new (next period's) target T_n is set according to

$$T_n = T_0 + t[Q - T_0] \qquad 0 \leqslant t \leqslant 1 \qquad\qquad (5.5)$$

Equation (5.5) assumed symmetry between over and underfulfilment and furthermore it was assumed that:

$$\frac{\partial U}{\partial T_n} < 0 \qquad \text{and} \ \frac{\partial U}{\partial Q} \geqslant 0 \qquad\qquad\qquad (5.6)$$

It would now follow that as actual output increased so would B, and since $U = B$, utility would also increase.   But the increase of Q would be accompanied by an increase in T_n and hence so would the disutility of higher targets.   As successive new targets approached the capacity level of the enterprise the disutility would increase at an increasing rate reflecting the difficulty of achieving the higher targets.

FIGURE 5.1   Indifference curves and plans

New targets

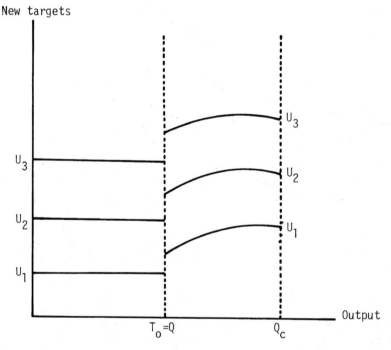

In order to combine these assumptions and variables in a single diagram Gindin devised an ingenious system of indifference curves. Consider U_1 in Figure 5.1. Up to $T_0 = Q$ the curve is flat indicating that there is no increase in bonus but also, to remain indifferent, no increase in targets. At $T_0 = Q$ bonus is received because the enterprise just fuflfils the target T_0, but also the target increases. There is a discontinuity in the curve indicating that the jump in the bonus is 'compensated' by the increase in the target. From Q to Q_c (capacity limit of the enterprise) bonuses increase and so do targets. The rate of substitution between bonus and targets increases at a decreasing rate indicating the disutility of the higher targets, or in other words smaller target increases are necessary to compensate the increases in output. The higher the indifference curve the less the level of utility, as the same level of output will be associated with a higher target. So it would follow that $U_1 >$ $U_2 > U_3$ in terms of levels of utility. Introducing the new target function (5.5) in Figure 5.1 may now yield the utility maximising level of output associated with the new target but also allow for the disutility of higher targets - a form of the ratchet effect. This is done in Figure 5.2. Different target functions are shown as T, T' etc.

FIGURE 5.2   Utility maximisation and plan fulfilment

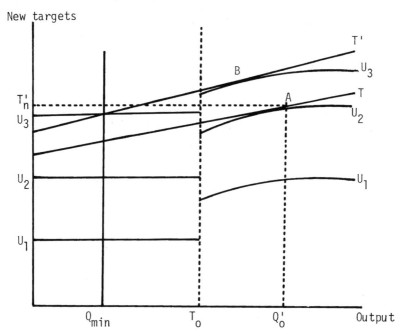

The tangency point at A in Figure 5.2 results in $Q_o' > T_o$ and a new target of T_n'. A change of the target function could have resulted to a tangency at B and a utility maximising level of output equalling zero! To avoid such unrealistic results a minimum level of output (say the level of output achieved in the previous period) can be built in to the model, for example Q_{min} in Figure 5.2.

An increase in the bonus paid for fulfilment of plan will shift all the indifference curves upwards lengthening the discontinuity. In Figure 5.2 if the enterprise is producing Q_{min} (i.e. a utility maximising position at a tangency point B), the increase in bonuses and the resulting shift of the indifference curves may lead to a new tangency to the right of B thus leading to an increase in output.

An increase in the targets however may lead to ambiguous results. The indifference curves will shift horizontally to the right and the target curve upwards. In Figure 5.3 if the utility maximising tangency was at point A, the increase in targets may lead to tangencies at either B, C or D thus leaving the level of output produced the same, increased or decreased. This diagram illustrates the case of an unchanged level of output produced. To compensate for this uncertainty of outcome the bonus for overfulfilment can be increased. This would increase the slope of the indifference curves (the dotted lines in Figure 5.3) thus leading to tangencies to the right of A.

FIGURE 5.3 Utility maximisation and changes in targets

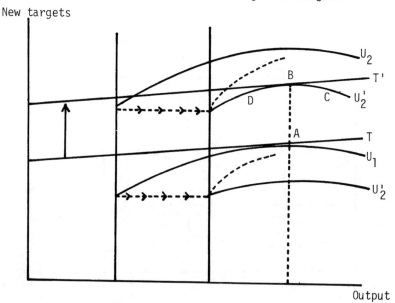

Gindin's analysis is interesting in that it illustrates the perennial problem facing planners in having to use the two instruments available to them to control enterprise behaviour; namely the change in plans and its uncertain effect on actual output and the manipulation of the bonus system in order to counteract the disutility of higher plans.

A further illustration of the static problem of designing incentive systems can be drawn from a model developed by Fan(5).

The bonus system was defined as

$$B = \alpha[Q_p + (1 - \epsilon)(Q - Q_p)] \qquad \text{for } Q > Q_p \qquad (5.7)$$

$$B = \alpha[Q_p + (1 + \epsilon)(Q - Q_p)] \qquad \text{for } Q < Q_p \qquad (5.8)$$

where Q and Q_p were actual and planned indexes (here output) and $0 < \alpha, \epsilon < 1$ fixed parameters. It would then follow that if $Q > Q_p$ the additional bonus per unit of output would be $\alpha(1 - \epsilon)$, whereas if the plan had been exactly fulfilled it would have been α.

If the maximum capacity of the enterprise was Q^* but the enterprise concealed this from the planners and reported $Q^* - C$ thus receiving $Q_p = Q^* - C$, then if $Q = Q^*$ the bonus would be

$$B = \alpha\left[(Q^* - C) + (1 - \epsilon)(Q^* - (Q^* - C))\right] \quad \text{or } B = \alpha Q^* - \epsilon C\alpha \qquad (5.9)$$

Had the enterprise reported its true capacity and produced to it (i.e. $Q_p = Q^*$ and $Q = Q^*$) then the bonus would have been

$$B = \alpha Q^*$$

which is clearly bigger than $B = \alpha Q^* - \epsilon C\alpha$. This system therefore penalises concealment and overfulfilment of plans thus approaching the desired specification of taut planning, i.e. ensuring that the bonus system encourages maximum output or at least produces accurate information as to true capacity.

Broadly similar results were obtained by assuming that Q^* and $Q^* - C$ were stochastic variables and then proceeding to estimate the conditions for maximising the expected level of bonuses.

These models are a step forward from the simple bonus maximising systems but they leave several points unexplored. In specific the actual plan does not appear to have any direct influence on enterprise behaviour as in, say, Hunter's hortatory effect. Neither does the potential problem of the ratchet principle is enlarged on, primarily because the analysis is static.

A pioneering attempt at the construction and empirical verification of a stochastic bonus function which allows for the role and importance of the plan in influencing enterprise behaviour was undertaken by Khaikin(6). This work is apparently unknown and unquoted in all western literature on this area but

Bonus Systems and Enterprise Behaviour

has been independently reproduced by various western authors. For this reason alone it merits some detailed examination.

Khaikin specified two bonus function for over and under-fulfilment of the plan (here assumed to be the output plan). The function for overfulfilment was expressed as:

$$B = \alpha Q_p + (Q - Q_p)\alpha k \qquad (5.10)$$

where the symbols have their usual meaning and coefficients α and k are $0 < \alpha$, k < 1. Expression (5.10) can be rewritten as

$$B = \alpha[Qk + Qp(1 - k)] \qquad (5.11)$$

with $(1 - k)$ standing for the 'penalty' for slack plans in the sense that if $Q > Q_p$ then the additional bonus for overfulfilment declined if α and k were given suitable numerical values. For underfulfilment the bonus formula was defined as

$$B^* = \alpha Q_p - \alpha Q_p \left(1 - \frac{Q}{Q_p}\right) m \qquad \text{with } m > 1$$

This also could be rewritten as

$$B^* = \alpha[Qm - (m - 1)Q_p] \qquad (5.12)$$

Khaikin then generalised his model by setting $\alpha = 1$ so that the bonus system could be written as

$$B = kQ + (1 - k)Q_p \quad \text{for overfulfilment} \qquad (5.13)$$

$$B^* = mQ - (m - 1)Qp \quad \text{for underfulfilment} \qquad (5.14)$$

The bonus for exactly fulfilling the plan would be $B = \alpha Q$ i.e. reverting back to the versions of the bonus formula in (5.11) and (5.12).

If now Q, the actual output or any other chosen index, is a stochastic variable with a density function P(Q) the expected value of the bonus can be written as

$$E(B) = \int_0^{Q_p} [mQ - (m-1)Q_p]P(Q)\,dQ + \int_{Q_p}^{\infty} [kQ + (1-k)Q_p]P(Q)\,dQ \qquad (5.15)$$

with $\int_0^{\infty} P(Q)\,dQ = 1$

Maximising (5.15) with respect to Q_p and rearranging gives

$$\int_{0}^{Q_p} P(Q)\,dQ = \frac{1-k}{m-k} \qquad (5.16)$$

This expression can be interpreted as follows: the level of output plan Q_p, call this Q_p^*, which will maximise the expected bonus must be such that for each marginal increase in that plan the bonus should increase by $1-k/m-k$. Given however that

$$m - k = (m - 1) + (1 - k)$$

i.e. the two expressions in the ratio are the penalties for under or overfulfilling the plan in terms of the additional bonuses lost or gained, then the ratio can be interpreted as

$$\frac{\text{Penalty in bonus for insufficiently taut plan}}{\text{Total penalties}}$$

Khaikin then proceeded to introduce an actual statistical distribution in order to obtain some numerical results for the bonus maximising formula. Using 11,000 monthly observations from seven enterprises producing cars, electrical transformers, generators and mining equipment over a 3-4 year period and covering the degree of fulfilment of plans for output, labour, productivity, wages fund, costs etc, several distributions of actual plan performance were obtained. On the basis of these observations the author felt confident enough to approximate the distribution of Q (or any other index used in planning) by a normal distribution.

Khaikin's analysis at this level, despite his rather heroic assumptions, is far more interesting for the methodology rather than its accuracy of results. After all, exact specification of a non-normal distribution would still allow predictions to be made except that the numerical calculations would be considerably more complex.

$F(t)$ was defined as being the probability distribution function of levels of Q (the actual output) that would just about fulfil the plan. $F(t)$ was also assumed to be normally distributed. The value of t was then normalised as:

$$t = \frac{Q - \bar{Q}}{\sigma}$$

with $\bar{Q}$ being the expected (average) level of fulfilled production and σ the average standard deviation. As the exercise however was concerned with the bonus maximising level of Q_p^* then $Q_p^* = Q$ was substituted in the normalised formula. This was justified on the basis that what the model was trying to solve for was a level of plan that if fulfilled would have maximised bonus. It then followed that:

$$t = \frac{Q_p^* - \bar{Q}}{\sigma} \quad \text{or} \quad Q_p^* = t\sigma + \bar{Q} \qquad (5.17)$$

and from (5.16), given the assumption of the distribution of $F(t)$

$$F(t) = \frac{1 - k}{m - k} \qquad (5.18)$$

Expressions (5.17) and (5.18) could then be used to produce numerical values for Q_p^* (7).

It is interesting to note from expression (5.17) that as long as $t > 0$ then $Q_p^* > \bar{Q}$ i.e. the optimum plan will bigger than expected level of output. It also follows that given the statistical distribution of Q the size of the plan that will maximise expected bonus will vary as the coefficients m and k vary. In other words if the enterprise is assumed to be bonus maximising the planners by varying the size of the co-efficients may make the enterprise change the size of the plan they may pursue or wish to achieve.

The model and its conclusions are of course simplistic as they depend on the assumptions that enterprises are bonus max-imisers, that the statistical distribution is normal and that planners are willing and able to change the bonus function co-efficients. There is of course the additional problem that Q_p^* has no normative significance as far as efficiency of resource allocation is concerned as the analysis is not exploring opti-mality nor it addresses itself to the problem of plan consist-ency within sectors or economy-wise. It is nonetheless an interesting exercise and represents an advance in Soviet micro-economics both because this is a model with an explicit behav-ioural assumption and because some of its empirical consequences are examined using actual data.

Khaikin's pioneering effort can now be used as the starting point in order to introduce and summarise a number of models developed by western authors. These models follow fairly closely Khaikin's basic tenets but are more sophisticated and in some cases, more realistic.

Using the assumption that enterprise managers are bonus maximisers, Bonin(8) developed the following stochastic model. Defining the bonus function as

$$B = \alpha \left(Q - \beta(Q - Qp) \right), \quad \alpha \text{ and } \beta \text{ being given constants}$$

with Q having a density function $f(Q)$, then the expected size of the bonus would be $E(B) = \alpha E(Q) - \beta E(Q - Q_p)$. Maximising $E(B)$ is formally equal to minimising with respect to Q_p:

$$E(B) = \int_{Q_p}^{\infty} (Q - Q_p) f(Q) dQ - \int_{0}^{Q_p} (Q - Q_p) f(Q) dQ \qquad (5.19)$$

The first expression shows the expected increase in bonus if $Q > Qp$, the second, the decrease if $Qp > Q$. Differentiating (5.19) with respect to Q_p and solving for the minimising value Q_p^* gives:

$$2F(Q_p^*) = 1 \quad \text{or}$$

$$F(Q_p^*) = \tfrac{1}{2} \tag{5.20}$$

where $F(Q_p^*)$ is the cumulative distribution of Q. It would then follow that the value of Q_p, Q_p^*, that will maximise the expected size of the bonus is equal to the median value of the distribution of the target, here output Q. The result is interesting because at this simple level, it is independent of the probabilistic distribution of Q. The system can be modified to discourage overfulfilment by a differentiated system of bonus weights, α^* and β^*, i.e.

$$B = \alpha[Q - \alpha^*(Q - Qp)] \quad \text{if } Q \geqslant Qp$$

$$B = \alpha[Q + \beta^*(Q - Qp)] \quad \text{if } Q \leqslant Qp$$

The E(B) expression now becomes

$$E(B) = \alpha E(Q) - \alpha \left[\alpha^* \int_{Q_p}^{\infty} (Q - Q_p) f(Q) dQ - \beta^* \int_{0}^{Q_p} (Q - Q_p) f(Q) dQ \right] \tag{5.21}$$

Maximising with respect to Qp is equivalent to minimising the expression in the square brackets. The result is

$$F(Q_p^*) = \frac{\alpha^*}{\alpha^* + \beta^*} \tag{5.22}$$

Comparing this expression with (5.20) it follows, that depending on whether $\alpha^* \gtrless \beta^*$, then $Q_p^* \gtrless Q_m$, Q_m being the median value of Q. It would also of course follow that if Q_p^* was the value that the enterprises themselves suggested then variation in the size of α^* and β^* would elicit different proposals from the enterprises. Rewriting (5.22) as

$$F(Q_p^*) = \frac{r}{r+1}, \quad \text{with } r = \frac{\alpha^*}{\beta^*}$$

then the probability that Q_p^* will be at least fulfilled is given by

$$1 - F(Q_p^*) = 1 - \frac{r}{r+1} = \frac{1}{r+1} \tag{5.23}$$

By setting $r < 1$ for enterprises high on priority of producing inputs widely used, the planners will expect on the average a better than 50-50 chance of that particular target being ful-

filled. This particular incentives scheme indicates that differentiated norms may assist to some extent with plan consistency, but that is, of course, dependent to some degree on knowledge of the statistical distribution, or at least on the assumption that the distribution of Q is similar amongst different
sectors. It is interesting to note that the models expounded
so far produced an important result in terms of planned tautness
- namely that the optimum plan may well be bigger than the
expected level of fulfilment. In other words either the enterprises or the planners will be willing to accept or to hand down
plans that are likely to be underfulfilled.

Before outlining the final and most recent stage in the
development of stochastic incentive schemes it is important to
draw attention to a number of changes in the Soviet bonus system that took place in the early 1970s. These changes caused a
partial shift of emphasis away from the purely static problem
of encouraging enterprises to reveal their true productive capacity towards the dynamic problem of the ratchet effect. These
changes and the resultant bonus system in current use are described in greater detail in Chapter 6. Briefly, however, the
idea was to encourage enterprises to put forward their own
counter-plans to those of the planners but penalise them
financially if they over or underfulfilled them or over or
underfulfilling the original plans in the absence of counter-
plans. The ratchet effect was to have been partially alleviated
by setting stable and unchanging targets over the FYP period.
It was thus hoped that encouraging the enterprises to put forward counter-plans would have yielded greater information on
their productive etc. capacity, but with given stable targets
the enterprises would not have been immediately faced with
higher planned targets for the next planning period.

A series of models and extensions on this particular scheme
were developed by Weitzman and Snowberger. It is important to
draw attention to the fact that although these models are an
approximation to the actual Soviet practice they are the near-
est to a realistic interpretation of the current situation in
the Soviet Union available at present.(9)

Enterprises receive at the beginning of the planning period
an output plan Q_p and a planned level of bonus fund B_p. The
final size of the bonus fund will depend not only on B_p but
also on the degree of exact/over/underfulfilment of Q_p and/or of
the counter-plan Q_p^c put forward by the enterprise.

If the enterprise suggests a counter-plan $Q_p^c > Q_p$ then the
potential bonus $\hat{B}$ will be

$$\hat{B} = B_p + \beta(Q_p^c - Q_p) \qquad (5.24)$$

The actual bonus, B, will depend on the relationship of actual
output Q to Q_p^c. So for overfulfilment, i.e. $Q > Q_p^c$ the bonus
will be

$$B = \hat{B} + \alpha(Q - Q_p^c) \qquad (5.25)$$

For underfulfilment $Q < Q_p^c$

$$B = \hat{B} - \gamma(Q_p^c - Q) \tag{5.26}$$

Since by definition

$$\hat{B} = B_p + \beta(Q_p^c - Q_p) \text{ then (5.25) can be written as}$$

$$B = B_p + \beta(Q_p^c - Q_p) + \alpha(Q - Q_p^c) \tag{5.27}$$

and (5.26) as

$$B = B_p + \beta(Q_p^c - Q_p) - \gamma(Q_p^c - Q) \tag{5.28}$$

If also $0 < \alpha < \beta < \gamma$ then the desired effect of encouraging exact plan fulfilment can be achieved.

With Q being a stochastic variable with a density function $f(Q)$, the expected bonus, $E(B)$, is

$$E(B) = \int_{-\infty}^{Q_p^c} \left[B_p + \beta(Q_p^c - Q_p) - \gamma(Q_p^c - Q) \right] f(Q) dQ$$

$$+ \int_{Q_p^c}^{+\infty} \left[B_p + \beta(Q_p^c - Q_p) + \alpha(Q - Q_p^c) \right] f(Q) dQ \tag{5.29}$$

$E(B)$ can now be maximised with respect to Q_p^c giving:

$$\frac{\partial E(B)}{\partial Q_p^c} = \int_{Q_p^c}^{\infty} f(Q) dQ = \frac{\gamma - \beta}{\gamma - \alpha} \tag{5.30}$$

Expression (5.30) can be interpreted in terms of the probability of actual output Q being bigger than or equal to the counter-plan level Q_p^c i.e.

$$P(Q \geqslant Q_p^c) = \frac{\gamma - \beta}{\gamma - \alpha} \tag{5.31}$$

It now follows that by increasing α, decreasing β or increasing γ the planners could induce enterprises to put forward smaller counter-plans in the expectation of an increased optimal over-fulfilment as it would pay to postpone revealing the true prod-uctivity capacity. Reversing the action would encourage ent-erprises to put forward higher, and therefore more ambitious targets, but with a potentially lower probability of fulfilling them. There are here some obvious similarities with Khaikin's results [see equation (5.16)] except that Khaikin's model did not contain the effects of expected bonuses from counter-plan Q_p^c.

Bonus Systems and Enterprise Behaviour

A further extension of the model can be derived by specifying risk aversion in terms of

$$\text{Max } EU(B) = EU(B_1) + EU(B_2)$$

with B_1 and B_2 being equations (5.28) and (5.27). The first order conditions for maximising expected bonus with respect to Q_p^c can now be obtained as

$$(\gamma - \beta) \int_{-\infty}^{Q_p} U'(B_1)\, f(Q)\, dQ = (\beta - \alpha) \int_{Q_p^c}^{\infty} U'(B_2)\, f(Q)\, dQ \qquad (5.32)$$

The signs of

$$\frac{\partial Q_p^c}{\partial \alpha} \text{ and } \frac{\partial Q_p^c}{\partial \gamma}$$

were both negative since by definition $U' > 0$, $U'' < 0$ with respect to the total size of bonus. Hence the enterprise's counterplan will decrease as the relative 'penalty' for over or underfulfilment in terms of bonuses increases. The signs of

$$\frac{\partial Q_p^c}{\partial \beta} \text{ or of } \frac{\partial Q_p^c}{\partial Q_p}$$

were not certain.

The Weitzman-Snowberger model predicts that manipulation of the bonus function coefficients can induce higher plans on the part of the enterprises but only at the expense of a lower probability of fulfilling them. Incorporating managerial effort in the production function can, however, change these predictions. This was done by Miller and Thornton.(10) Managers can now be induced by an appropriate change in the bonus function coefficients to increase their targets. This may also increase, rather than decrease, the probability of fulfilling them. There is a problem however in that the disutility of effort will determine the actual level of output as managers try more (or less) hard to fulfil their targets. It now follows that planners will be unable to know, or even guess, the probability of an enterprise fulfilling its plan because the cost of the disutility of effort will be subjective and therefore not measurable. An extension of the model to two periods and the inclusion of the ratchet effect predicted that managers will benefit if they do not attempt to produce at their maximum capacity.

As the ratchet effect and its interaction with the incentive schemes is essentially a dynamic problem, the models described so far can be made even more realistic and afford a more accurate insight into the Soviet planning problems by considering the effects of these bonus functions on managerial behaviour over time. Murrell(11) extended a model similar to those of Fan, Bonin, and Weitzman into a multi-period framework. Managers can now carry over undeclared inventories from period to period if they wish to hide the true extent of their current performance. For a manager with a certain type of time preference as expressed in his rate of time discount, given the coefficients of the bonus function, the incentive scheme could induce an accurate report of the achieved output and no undeclared, hidden inventories of goods. But for a different pattern of time preferences, and therefore discount rates, it can be shown that managers may prefer to keep some output as undeclared inventories. In this case managers will have to evaluate the benefits of an honest declaration of the output achieved against keeping it as hidden inventories. This decision will influence what targets are then likely to be set for the enterprise for the next period. Furthermore, Murrell goes on to show that it is possible to envisage a situation where the planners will be unable to induce managers to either suggest a realistic target or make them report the true level of production or of other accomplishments. It can now be seen that the bonus scheme developed so far may encourage 'honest reporting' of capacity in the sense that managers will be willing to reveal in a counter proposal or target their true productive capacity. The ratchet effect however will appear in whether or not they will be willing to report accurately what they have achieved.

Lin(12) extended Murrel's analysis to show that in a two-period situation changes in the bonus function coefficients could induce honest reporting of achievement as long as managers had a preference for present day income over future. If they did not they could still tend to conceal the achieved results.

The ratchet effect implies a penalty in terms of potentially foregone future bonuses as successive planned targets increase and therefore become more difficult to fulfil. It should be possible to quantify this penalty in the context of a multi-period bonus function and by varying its monetary value, affect both the actual performance of the enterprise and therefore plans handed to it, as long as they were based on the last actual reported performance. The whole principle of the ratchet effect depends on the assumption that future higher plans will be more difficult, or less likely, to achieve. It is now possible to turn this into an equivalent statement in terms of future plans being tauter. After all an increase in a target which is not followed by an increase in all the necessary inputs and other requirements to fulfil it, can be deemed as equivalent to the target remaining the same but the enterprise being allocated fewer resources to fulfil it. This may sound contradictory in the context of the bonus function which has been used so far which requires higher targets and fulfilment in order for more money to be paid as bonuses. But it is important to remember that Soviet enterprises can, and are set, targets to reduce the cost of production, to increase profitability of cap-

ital used or economise in the use of materials. All these targets may involve using less of inputs to achieve either the same
or higher level of output, hence a tauter plan.

Use of elementary techniques of optimum control methods
yields some interesting results and insights into this multi-
period maximising problem.(13) Assume a general bonus function:

$$B = B(Q,N,t) \qquad (5.33)$$

where Q, the state variable can be any of the planned indexes
used, here output, N being the control variable standing for
some measure of tautness, and t being time. The enterprise
manager is then expected to maximise

$$\int_t^{t'} B(Q,N,t)\, e^{-rt}\, dt \qquad (5.34)$$

where t→t' can be either the five years of the plan or any other
specified time period. The state variable Q can be defined
either as:

$$\frac{dQ}{dt} = N \qquad (5.35)$$

or in a general form

$$\frac{dQ}{dt} = f(Q,N,t) \qquad (5.36)$$

Forming now the Hamiltonian using (5.35)

$$H = e^{-rt}\, [B(Q,N,t) + \lambda(t)\, N] \qquad (5.37)$$

and using one of the necessary conditions for maximisation from
the canonical equations:

$$\frac{d\lambda}{dt} = -\frac{\partial H}{\partial Q} \quad \text{and}$$

$$\frac{d\lambda}{dt} e^{-rt} - \lambda(t)re^{-rt} = \frac{\lambda B}{\lambda Q} e^{-rt} \quad \text{or} \qquad (5.38)$$

$$-\frac{d\lambda}{dt} = B_Q - \lambda(t)r \qquad (5.39)$$

Similarly using specification (5.36) the conditions are

$$-\frac{d\lambda}{dt} = B_Q - \lambda(t)(r - f_Q) \qquad (5.40)$$

Equations (5.39) and (5.40) can be interpreted as follows:
the Lagrangean multiplier λ is the opportunity cost of a unitary
relaxation of the tautness control variable in terms of bonuses.
It then follows that a fall in the opportunity cost of tautness

130

over a short period of time must equal the net increase in bonuses resulting from an increase in output. It also follows from the necessary conditions of N being a maximising value that $\partial H/\partial N = 0$ if N attains a maximum value at a certain N, N*. So from (5.35) and (5.36):

$$B_N = -\lambda(t) \tag{5.41}$$

$$B_N = -\lambda(t)f_N \tag{5.42}$$

It follows from (5.41) and (5.42) that the additional bonus earned by increases in tautness must be balanced with the negative effect of the decisions taken today on the future level of bonuses. Solutions of the optimising path of output and degree of tautness can be found by specifying the relevant functions. Since tautness however is best defined in stochastic terms, the problem then becomes quite difficult as it would require some assumptions about the probabilistic distribution of N.

Weitzman(14) developed a somewhat similar model except that he was able to express the cost of the ratchet effect directly in terms of actual bonus coefficients and also to indicate the effect of the variations of these costs on the optimum output of the enterprise.

The enterprise is expected to maximise the present day (i.e. discounted) net value of its bonuses. The bonus function is specified very simply as:

$$B = b(Q_t - Q_{pt}) \tag{5.43}$$

with b as the bonus coefficient and the rest of the symbols having their usual meaning, i.e. Q being the actual and Q_p the planned level of putput (or other targets) with the addition of the subscript t standing for the appropriate time period. The simplification of the bonus function is compared to the elaborate formulas of expressions (5.27) and (5.28) above does not diminish the usefulness of the exercise as Weitzman was preoccupied not with the static properties of the systems, i.e. whether it encourages the managers to reveal true capacities via counter-plans, but with the dynamic ones, i.e. whether present performance would influence future performance as perceived by the managers. A change of plan function incorporating the ratchet effect was specified as:

$$Q_{pt} - Q_{pt-1} = \delta_t + \phi_t(Q_{t-1} - Q_{pt-1}) \tag{5.44}$$

with δ_t representing by how much the target would have changed in period t if the last period's targets had been met exactly. But for every extra unit or percentage point that the performance of the last period exceeded the planned level, today's plan will increase by an extra ϕ_t. The adjustment coefficient ϕ_t is treated as a 'behavioural parameter of the planner that quantifies the strength of the ratchet principle'. Expression (5.44) is then rewritten in terms of Q_{pt} and then substituted into (5.43). Finally, there is a cost function in terms of the disutility that is incurred when the enterprise decides to produce Q at period t

$$C = C(Q_t, E_t) \qquad (5.45)$$

where E_t is a random variable known at time t but unknown before which characterises costs or technical conditions of the enterprise during period t.

The enterprise then is assumed to maximise the expected net present day value of bonuses, that is the difference between the expected present day value of (5.43) and (5.45). The enterprise is also assumed to have an explicit time preference as expressed in the discount rate, r, used. Weitzman solves the problem by finding the optimal level of output Q_t^* that the enterprise should produce in successive time periods. This is done in terms of a marginal cost rule, i.e. the optimum output is obtained at the point where its marginal cost is equal to

$$\frac{b}{1 + \frac{\phi}{r}} \qquad (5.46)$$

This can be interpreted as a 'ratchet price' in the sense that if the enterprise was asked to maximise

$$P^*Q_t - C(Q_t, E_t)$$

where P* equals the expression (5.46), then it would produce automatically the optimum output Q_t^* by the simple expedient of setting marginal costs equal to P*. It would now follow that the higher the P* the higher would be the optimal output in each time period. This result does make intuitive sense because as Weitzman observes

> ... the ratchet price is essentially the bonus coefficient b adjusted by a term ϕ/r which captures the effect of the ratchet on future plan quotas and enterprise bonuses' (The Ratchet Principle ... p.306)

Dynamic planning and optimum control methods can offer a further insight into the operations of the Soviet enterprise especially on the ratchet effect of planning and its interaction with the incentive system. At the same time however the survey of the existing literature points out to the yet unresolved problem of the static and dynamic problem of incentives. Expressing the ratchet effect in terms of a price offers an elegant illustration and a possible quantitative solution but it does leave unanswered the question of the determinants of the discount rate used by enterprises. If this is an implicit rate expressing individual preferences and therefore purely subjective, then these models are not any nearer to offering firm predictions on performance and reactions to changes in plans.

What is possibly a more serious criticism is that the models developed so far do not show or predict what will happen to the actual level of output or any other target of the enterprise. This is not surprising as these models were developed to solve either for the centrally determined plans or for the counter-plans that would maximise bonuses. Whether the actual output will equal the planned will now depend on the factors that can be controlled by the enterprise and on those that cannot. The former will include input reserves, levels of X-efficiency as well as the counter-plan itself. The latter will include the stochastic influences on Q such as the unreliability of the supply system. The argument taken to its logical conclusion does imply that in a perfect and certain world the bonus maximising enterprise would end up producing its counter-plan, if it has put one forward.

5.3 SUMMARY AND CONCLUSIONS

The implications of the material presented so far can now be summarised under three headings:

Firstly, the actual form of the bonus functions is likely to affect the plans that the enterprise managers are willing to put forward and/or accept subject, however, to the degree of uncertainty involved. In most cases the size of the bonus coefficients is of crucial importance in determining whether on the average the planned level of output will be bigger than the expected level of plan fulfilment. This can be interpreted in two different ways: The planners by varying the size of the coefficients may be able to influence the counter-plans that enterprises suggest and thus exert a varying degree of pressure on their productive capacity. Furthermore, the results give an approximate numerical value of the degree of planned tautness in the sense that there might be cases where the planned level of targets must be bigger than the expected level of actual fulfilment if the bonuses are to be maximised.

Secondly, the parametric control of enterprise behaviour via the bonus system coefficients appear to be a far more promising way of establishing a method whereby greater information can be obtained of the productive capacity of the enterprise. The major practical snag however of this approach is that the current Soviet practice dictates a general uniformity of the 'coefficients of deduction' (i.e. coefficients in the bonus functions) amongst most branches of industry and the implicit promise that these coefficients will remain fixed for the duration of the FYP in order to allow enterprises to plan and execute their targets with a relative degree of certainty. In other words the current Soviet practice precludes frequent changes of these coefficients of deduction. Whether this does happen or not in practice is an empirical question; there is ample evidence however that even if the bonus coefficients stay unchanged the plans do not. Furthermore, the practicality of attempting to control enterprise behaviour over time by changing bonus function coefficients will be seriously compromised if the enterprises are subjected to the same treatment they are with plan changes. That is, if the bonus coefficients are changed in order to ensure that all enterprises earn reasonable bonuses irrespective of their performance. Even if that did not happen it is highly unlikely that Soviet planners and managers alike would wish to add to the existing uncertainty over the outcome of their operations by changes in bonus function coefficients.

Finally, the systems outlined so far depend completely on the assumption that the enterprise managers are bonus maximisers. Whether this is true or not is an empirical question which depends both on the relative size of bonuses as a part of managerial earnings and also on the degree of the relationship between the size of the bonus, the level of planned targets and the actual performance. Judgement on these important points is reserved until the next chapter.

Notes

1. P. Wiles, Economic Institutions Compared, Basil Blackwell, Oxford 1977, p.63.

2. M.L. Weitzman, 'The "Ratchett" Principle and Performance Incentives', The Bell Journal of Economics, Vol.11, No. 1, Spring 1980, pp.302-3. For a general introduction to the incentives problems see M. Cave and P. Hare, Alternative Approaches to Economic Planning, Macmillan, London 1981, Ch.9 passim.

3. W.A. Leeman, 'Bonus Formulae and Soviet Managerial Performance', Southern Economic Journal, Vol.36, March 1970, pp.434-45. See also the comments on Leeman's article by F.W. Rushing, Southern Economic Journal, Vol.38, April 1972, pp.569-72 and by M. Ellman, Southern Economic Journal, Vol.39, April 1973, pp.652-53.

4. S. Gindin, A Model of the Soviet Firm, Economics of Planning, Vol.10, No.3, 1970, pp.145-57.

5. L.S. Fan, 'On the Reward Systems', American Economic Review, Vol.65, March 1975, pp.226-29.

6. V.P. Khaikin, Plan i Material' noe stimulirovanie, Moscow 1970, passim, but especially Chs.1-3.

7. Khaikin derived the following example. He sets $m = 3$, $k = 0.7$, $Q = 100$ and $\sigma = 2$, which using expression (5.18) gave

Bonus Systems and Enterprise Behaviour

$$F(t) = \frac{1 - 0.7}{3 - 0.7} = 0.13$$

The figure 0.13 corresponded, always according to Khaikin's own calculations, to a normalised $t = -1.13$. This t value was then substituted in expression (5.17) which produced an expected bonus maximising Q_p:

$$Q_p^* = -1.13(2) + 100 = 97.74.$$

This can be interpreted as follows: from the point of view of the enterprise, given the numerical values of the parameters and the characteristics of the statistical distribution of Q, if the plan that the enterprise receives and tries to achieve is about 97% of the expected level of fulfilled output or other targets, then the expected bonus will be maximised.

8. J.P. Bonin, 'On the Design of Managerial Incentives Structures in a Decentralized Planning Environment', American Economic Review, Vol.66, Sept. 1976, pp.682-87.

9. M.L. Weitzman, The New Soviet Incentive Model, The Bell Journal of Economics, Vol.7, No.1, Spring 1976, pp.251-57; V. Snowberger, The New Soviet Incentive Model: Comment, The Bell Journal of Economics, Vol.8, No.2, Autumn 1977, pp.591-600. See also V. Snowberger, 'The Interaction between Central Planners and Firms: The Uncertainty of Target Adjustment' in Economics of Planning, Vol.15, Nos.2-3, 1979, pp.168-83.

10. J.B. Miller and J.R. Thornton, 'Effort, Uncertainty and the New Soviet Incentive System', Southern Economic Journal, Vol.45, No.2, October 1978, pp.432-46.

11. P. Murrell, 'The Performance of Multi-Period Managerial Incentive Schemes', American Economic Review, Vol.69, No. 5, December 1979, pp.934-40.

12. Chao-Nan Lin, 'The Ratchet Principle: A Diagrammatic Interpretation', Journal of Comparative Economics, Vol.6, No.1, March 1982, pp.75-80.

13. The dynamic exposition here is based on D. Koo, Elements of Optimization, Springer-Verlag, New York 1977, Ch.8, and on A.P. Jacquemin and J. Thisse, Strategy of the Firm and Market Structure: An Application of Optimal Control Theory, in K. Cowling (Ed.), Market Structure and Corporate Behaviour, Gray Mills, London 1972, pp.62-84. See also the general survey on related issues contained in E. Ekman, Dynamic Economic Models of the Firm, Economic Research Institute, (EFI), Stockholm, 1978.
J.A. Yunker in 'A Dynamic Optimization Model of the Socialist Enterprise', Economics of Planning, Vol.13, No.1-2, 1973, pp.35-51, used a managerial utility function which contained bonuses as an argument and which allowed for the ratchet effect of overfulfilment. The article explored the conditions under which the plan would be exactly fulfilled but did not offer any conclusions of operational significance.

14. Weitzman, The Ratchet Principle and Performance Incentives, pp.302-8.

135

Chapter Six

INCENTIVES FUNDS AND BONUSES

6.1 INTRODUCTION

This chapter outlines in some detail the system of incentives
and bonus schemes currently applicable in the Soviet Union for
the eleventh FYP (1981-85).   The aim here is to link together
within an institutional and factual framework the material presented in Chapters 4 and 5 and to appraise the quantitative
evidence of the role of incentives as parameters affecting enterprise behaviour. The first section outlines the rules governing the formation of the Material Incentive Fund (MIF). The
next section examines the formation of various other bonus
schemes, and the following two sections appraise the available
Soviet statistical and econometric evidence on the role and influence of these funds and bonuses. All these findings are then
summarised.
       It is very important at the outset to clarify in some de-
tail the area that will be surveyed.
       Firstly, the incentive schemes to be examined in Section
6.2 are designed in order to influence the decision-making of
the managerial and white-collar staff. The sources of funds for
these schemes are the profits of the enterprise. The major aim
of the schemes is to encourage the enterprise to put forward
their own higher but realisable counter-plans, especially of
output. In a sense, the enterprises are expected to impose on
themselves a degree of tautness, since the counter plan does not
entitle them to any further input allocated by the Gossnab.
There is a host of subsidiary targets at which incentive schemes
also aim - such as technological innovation, the saving of
energy, the slowing down of labour turnover etc. All these are
examined in Section 6.3. The quantitative significance of these
particular bonus schemes will be examined as well, but the main
emphasis will be on the role of the incentive schemes and taut
planning as defined above.(1)
       Secondly, the incentive schemes and in particular the Mat-
erial Incentives Fund (MIF) which is examined in detail in
Section 6.2 is primarily designed with the managerial and white-

collar staff in mind. This is so because bonuses from MIF
account for a relatively low proportion of total bonuses received by workers and also because of the rules concerning its
formation and disbursement that tend to put the onus for certain aspects of plan fulfilment on managerial rather than purely
'production effort' criteria. This is particularly true where
the planned targets are the assortment plans and the percentage
of high quality good to total output, i.e. targets that rely on
decisions as to what to produce rather than overall level of
output. This is not to say of course that production workers
are not directly involved or motivated by the potential bonuses
receivable from the MIF. It is important however to emphasise
that production workers can, and do, receive payments that resem-
ble or are bonuses but which strictly speaking do not come under
the category of payments to be discussed in Section 6.2. Industrial workers may receive payments over and above the official
wage rate or the piece rates where these apply, for fulfilling
for example production norms or raising labour productivity.
These additional payments are unrelated to the incentive schemes
and any bonus received under examination in Section 6.2 because:

(a) they are paid out of the wages fund and not out of the
     profits or special bonus funds,
(b) they are not necessarily linked to planned vs actual per-
     formance or counter-plans in the sense that planned taut-
     ness will not affect their size,
(c) these bonuses are paid to workers only - whereas the in-
     centive schemes to be examined here include managerial
     staff as well as workers.

     In appraising however the significance of the incentive
funds both as part of the industrial-productive personnel and
of their influence on decision-making, it will be made clear in
the text - where necessary or relevant - which premia or bonuses
derive from profits or special funds.(2)

6.2 THE PRESENT SYSTEM OF MATERIAL INCENTIVES FUND:
     A CRITICAL APPRAISAL

The major source of incentives funds for the Soviet enterprise
for the eleventh FYP (1981-85) is the Material Incentives Fund
(MIF). The fund is formed out of the enterprise's profits. As
the rules that govern its formation and distribution are rather
complex, and therefore tedious to describe in detail, it will
be useful to outline first the absolute barest essential of the
scheme in operation for the eleventh FYP and then fill in the
details as necessary.(3) This will be done in four steps.
     Firstly, the indexes that govern the formation of the plan
are the set targets for the growth of labour productivity and
the percentage of high quality goods to total output. There are

two exceptions however. For light, food, dairy and fish industries an alternative index can be used, that of output in value
terms. For mining industries the planned output may be expressed in physical units rather than in value terms.   As will be
shown later on, enterprises can be set additional targets to
fulfil and these may increase or decrease the MIF. The official
literature however makes it clear that the most important fund-
forming indexes are the growth of labour productivity and the
percentage of high quality goods produced.

Secondly, the actual MIF receivable by the enterprise is
based on planned MIF and on whether the associations or enterprises offer any counter-plans to the official plans and degree
to which these plans are fulfilled. The MIF is of course paid
out of net profits, but in order to determine its actual size
it has to be expressed as a percentage of a certain sum of
money. For the eleventh FYP this is the level of planned profits, except that for the light etc. industries the 1980 wages
fund is used instead. So now the actual MIF that the enterprise will receive will be equal to

$$\text{MIF}_{(Actual)} = \text{MIF}_{(Planned)} \pm \text{Profits (or Wages Fund 1980)} \times$$

[Coefficients of deduction depending on degree of plan
 fulfilment.]

Even this scheme is over-simplified because:

(a) $\text{MIF}_{(Planned)}$ depends on whether there are any counter-
     plans to the FYP handed down by Gosplan.
(b) The degree of over/underfulfilment of either the original
     or the counter-plans.

Thirdly, the planned MIF is determined as follows.   The
control figures handed down to the ministries and association,
contains a figure for the initial planned level of MIF,denoted
here as MIFp, for the whole of the FYP as well as for the individual years. The official literature is completely silent on
what determines this initial planned size of MIF.(4) Given the
control figures on the planned rate of growth of labour productivity and the percentage of high quality goods to total output,
the following two ratios are then calculated.

$$Z_L = \left[\frac{\text{MIF}_P}{\substack{\text{Planned Profit} \\ \text{(control figures)}}} \right] \left[\frac{100}{\substack{\text{Rate of growth of labour productivity} \\ \text{(control figures)}}} \right]$$

$$Z_G = \left[\frac{\text{MIF}_P}{\substack{\text{Planned Profit} \\ \text{(control figures)}}} \right] \left[\frac{100}{\substack{\text{Percentage of high quality goods} \\ \text{(control figures)}}} \right]$$

Exactly similar rules apply for the light etc. industries except

138

that the 1980 wage fund is used instead of planned profits. In
order to avoid unnecessary complications and repetitions the
rules concerning the light etc. industries will be ignored from
now on as they are almost identical to those applying to the
rest of the sectors.

These two Z coefficients can be interpreted as the proportion of planned profits weighted by the relevant success indicators that will be directed towards the planned MIF.

Before describing the scheme any further it will be useful
at this stage to reiterate an essential feature of the five-
yearly and annual planning cycle of the USSR. Ministries,
associations and their sub-ordinate enterprises are encouraged,
if not expected, to offer alternative, counter, plans to those
incorporated in the Gosplan control figures handed down to them.
There are, however, two types of counter-plan,

(a) offers of higher (or lower) plans to the control figures
    of the FYP;
(b) offers of higher (or lower) plans to those incoroporated
    in the annual versions of the FYP.

It is important to remember that the control figures established
for the FYP are split into their annual components, but these
annual plans are then effectively 'replanned' on a yearly basis
thus allowing the associations and enterprises to change or vary
the original estimates and counter-proposals to the control
figures. The term 'counter-plan' is used in the official Soviet
literature to indicate counter-proposals to the annual plans
rather than control figures. To avoid confusion however the term
counter-plan is used here without differentiation. In essence
this does not make any difference as the idea of the 'counter
proposal' is to encourage higher plans at every stage of the
planning process.

The Z coefficients derived above are then used to establish
a further version of MIF_p, the MIF_p^* on the basis of counter-
plans, if any, to the control figures. If there are no counter-
plans, then Z_L and Z_G are multiplied by the percentage increase
or proportions, of the established targets and by the level of
planned profits thus establishing the MIF_p^* for this stage of the
calculations. If there are counter-plans for the growth of
labour productivity, Z_L is increased by four times and is then
multiplied by the additional extra planned increase. If the
ministry or association had suggested a lower labour productivity plan then Z_L is increased by three times but is then used
to decrease MIF_p by the appropriate proportion. Similar rules
hold for the plans for high quality goods except that Z_G is not
used here. Instead, for every one per cent increase (decrease)
in the counter-plans the Planned MIF_p is increased (decreased)
by 4% (3%). To clarify these points it is important to emphasise that these counter-plans will increase (decrease) the already established MIF_p. So, for example, for the labour

Incentive Funds and Bonuses

productivity plan (where the subscripts L and G denote the appropriate plan and its effect on the size of MIF_p):

$$MIF^*_{PL} = Z_L \text{ [Planned increases x Planned Profits]} \pm$$

$$Z_L \text{ [4(or 3\%) Extra Increase (decrease) x Planned Profits]}$$

A similar formula holds for the high quality goods plan (G).

$$MIF^*_{PG} = Z_G \text{ [Planned Percentage x Planned Profits]} \pm MIF_p$$

$$\text{[4\% (or 3\%) x Extra Percentage Increase (decrease)]}$$

The figures for MIF^*_{PL} and MIF^*_{PG} are of course divided into their annual planned components thus establishing the level of the planned MIF following the counter-proposals, if any, to the control figures. The same formula is then applied to these figures that were used to derive the Z coefficients above, except that the MIF figures are now denoted by MIF^*_{PL} and MIF^*_{PG} and the original planned targets are the newly established ones (if any) rather than the original control figures. Call these new Z coefficients Z^*_L and Z^*_G.

The finalised yearly MIF plan is then constructed by using these new coefficients. If the associations or enterprises do not propose to change the plans negotiated initially over the control figures (and their yearly components), then the planned MIF for the year in question will be calculated by multiplying the level of planned profits for the year by the appropriate Z^*_L or Z^*_G coefficient times the rate of increase (or percentage) of the appropriate target.

If the enterprises are putting forward an annual plan which is different from that of the annual component of the five year plan, then for every additional 1% increase in labour productivity the Z^*_L will increase by three times and for every 1% increase in the proportion of high quality goods to the total output the MIF^*_{PG} will increase by 3%. If these annual counter-plans involve decreases in the targets as set out in the five-year plan then these coefficients will fall by no less than 10%. The Planned MIF will therefore increase or decrease accordingly.

Fourthly, and finally, the actual MIF receivable by the enterprise and used to pay out bonuses will now depend on the degree of fulfilment of the annual plans and counter-plans, if any. The figure that will emerge from the final stage of the calculations in the third step described above will be the planned MIF for the year in question. Call this MIF_Y. If the enterprise fulfils exactly all its plans for that year then the actual MIF received will equal MIF_Y. If the enterprise either over or underfulfils its plans the MIF_Y will increase or decrease. There are a number of possibilities here depending on whether there were any counter-plans and the degree of plan fulfilment in general:

(a) For the overfulfilment of any yearly plan target, including
     those of counter-plans the MIF$_\gamma$ will increase by an amount
     equal to

$$\begin{pmatrix} \text{Actual Profit} \\ \text{for that year} \end{pmatrix} \begin{pmatrix} \text{Per cent} \\ \text{overfulfilment} \end{pmatrix} \; Z_L^* \; (\text{or } Z_G^*)$$

The Z coefficients, however, will be decreased by no less
than 30%. In other words the extra MIF earned for plan
over-fulfilment will yield a smaller sum of money than the
enterprise would have made had it offered a higher plan
compared to the FYP targets and then fulfilled it exactly.

(b) In cases of under-fulfilment of the planned targets there
     are two possibilities:

(i) For enterprises that had established counter-plans
on labour productivity but under-fulfilled them, their
MIF$_\gamma$ will be reduced by increasing the coefficient Z_L^* by
no less than 30% and then following the procedure described in (a) above, except that the percentage will refer
to the underfulfilment of the plan.
     For the underfulfilment of high quality goods counter-
plans the MIF$_\gamma$ will decrease by 3 percentage points for
every 1% underfulfilment.
(ii) For enterprises with no counter-plans the MIF$_\gamma$ will
be decreased by applying the coefficients Z_L^* and Z_G^* to the
actual profits made and following the procedure in (a)
above except that these coefficients will be increased by
no less than 30% and the percentage will refer to the
underfulfilment.
     Underfulfilment in other words leads to proportionally
higher losses (penalties) on MIF earned.

In all cases of over or underfulfilment the exact numerical increase or decrease of the coefficients is determined by the appropriate ministry and the trade union.
     As already indicated the key success indicators for the
eleventh FYP are the growth in labour productivity and the percentage of high quality goods to the total output. There are,
however, a number of other targets or success indicators that
ministries can impose on associations and enterprises, such as
planned reductions in the cost of production, higher capital
productivity and profitability. Furthermore, some enterprises
might be assigned on an experimental basis Net Normed Production targets. There is, however, a general pre-condition
that the labour productivity target must be included and that
at least 50% of the planned MIF must be derived from the fulfilment of that target.
     Enterprises have also an assortment plan to fulfil.   For
those that fulfil theirs on a quarterly basis and on time, the
planned MIF for that period will increase by 10%.   If the

assortment plan is not fulfilled then the value of the goods involved will be excluded from the calculations determining the overall value of output of the enterprise. The implication of these provisions are that enterprises producing the wrong assortment of goods will not be able to claim that they have fulfilled their overall sales plan. In these cases of underfulfilling the assortment plans the MIF will be reduced by no less than 1% for every percentage point underfulfilment of the assortment plan. There are also additional rules concerning the output of high quality goods, profitability and above plan profits.

It is interesting to note that the rules concerning both formation of the MIF and the planned indexes used, do not include explicitly the total value of output or sales. The sales plan appears indirectly via the assortment plan. In other words the total sales plan, which is a planned target for the enterprise but not a fund-forming index, appears as far as the MIF formation is concerned as a number of assortment plans. Furthermore, profitability and labour productivity targets will be affected if the assortment plan is not fulfilled since the value of sales used in calculating these targets will exclude the value of underfulfilled assortment plans.

On first sight these specific rules concerning output and assortment may appear peculiar to observers used to treating the Soviet enterprises as output or sales maximisers. Cynics may well point out that what the MIF rules indicate is one thing and what the Ministries and enterprises will do is another. In other words the sales (output) target may still be the most important one for enterprises to fulfil. This assumption would be right in the unrealistic case where the enterprise produced only one type of good. Once the enterprises produce more than one type of good, the assortment plan can be easily substituted for the sales plan. This may well mean that in terms of plan discipline the enterprise still attempts to maximise the total sales and that the Ministry simply changes the assortment plan in order to accommodate any enterprise in danger of not fulfilling their plans.

It is important to note that there is nothing unusual in establishing the actual size of the MIF on the basis of a number of targets but then make the actual payment (or increases or decreases of its size) conditional on the fulfilment of a different set of targets. So for example although increase in labour productivity is likely to be a target that most enterprises will have to fulfil if their MIF is to be formed at all, underfulfilling their assortment plan will reduce the MIF, despite the fact that the assortment plan might not have been included in the targets that determined the size of the MIF in the first place. The MIF however cannot fall in any single year below 40% of the annual planned size. This rule is presumably a safety net for those enterprises that underfulfilled their plans but not necessarily through their own fault.

Incentive Funds and Bonuses

The Socio-cultural and Housing Fund is formed as a percentage of MIF (30 to 50%) and then is increased or decreased according to the degree of plan fulfilment as reflected on the MIF itself. The actual size of the coefficient used, i.e. whether 30% or up to 50% of MIF, is determined by the social needs of the enterprise involved, i.e. the state of the housing stock, the number of young children in the workers' families etc.

Once the MIF has been formed it will of course eventually be paid out to managers and workers. In general payments of bonuses are made on a quarterly basis with adjustments allowing for the varying degree of plan fulfilment over the year. The actual distribution of bonuses from the MIF amongst managers, white and blue collar workers and the production workers in general, is determined on the basis of a broad set of directives from the planners which are then elaborated by the individual ministries and enterprises in conjunction with the appropriate Trade Union.(5) The rules concerning the allocation of the MIF to managers and the engineering-technical workers (cyrillic initials ITR) and to production workers are clearly differentiated.(6)

Payment of bonuses from the MIF to workers will be made only if basic planned targets have been met i.e. growth of labour productivity and the percentage of high quality goods to total output. Workers or groups of workers are expected to fulfil no more than two or three basic plan indexes. In case of underfulfilment of these indexes bonus payments can be decreased by up to 50%. The payments of bonuses can be differentiated between groups of workers depending on whether some groups had accepted higher targets, fulfilled their allocated tasks in time and so on. The precise amount of the allocation will be determined by the enterprise and the appropriate Trade Union.

For managers the only source of bonuses is the MIF. This is not necessarily so for workers or ITR who may receive bonuses paid out of the wage fund as well as from the MIF. For managers only, bonus payments are conditional on the fulfilment of the two basic targets: labour productivity and high quality goods. Additional tasks can be imposed on managers before premia are paid out, such as fulfilment of the assortment plan. In cases of underfulfilment of targets the premia can be reduced by up to 50%. If the wage fund is overspent managers may face up to 50% premia losses as a penalty. The rules for ITR are broadly similar except that in general they tend to contain fewer provisos or penalty clauses in cases of breaches of plans. For both groups of managers and ITR however the premia receivable cannot exceed 50-60% of basic salary. In addition to this the average share of managers' premia cannot exceed that of the ITR and other salaried personnel and vice versa. The exact rules concerning all these payments are again subject to appropriate agreement between the enterprise, the supervisory organs and the Trade Unions.

From the description of the current Soviet incentives system it is apparent that the analytical schemes developed by Weitzman and Khaikin (see Chapter 5 passim) approximate in the abstract the contemporary Soviet practice. The aim of the bonus system now is to reward taut planning in the sense of encouraging the enterprises to put forward counter plans that they intend to fulfil exactly without at the same time making any further demands for inputs. In addition to this overfulfilment of either the original or of the counter-plan is discouraged since the additional MIF thus generated will be smaller than the case where the enterprise put forward a plan and then fulfilled it exactly. Similarly of course underfulfilment of plan generates higher penalties in terms of decreases in the size of the MIF especially when counterplans are underfulfilled. As has already been indicated one of the key problems facing planners in designing a bonus system is the elimination of the disincentive effect of the ratchet and simultaneously encouraging the enterprises to reveal their true productive capacity. This is the familiar dynamic and static problems of bonus design. Given that these problems bedevilled Soviet planners in their quest for a bonus function that eliminated them both, it may well be useful at this stage to outline briefly the basic element of bonus schemes in the 1960s and early 1970s and compare them to the present system. This will facilitate the appraisal of the degree by which these schemes were successful in dealing with the static and dynamic incentives problem. Indeed, recently authors have raised questions on whether the currently applicable systems for the tenth, and by extension for the eleventh FYPs, were significantly different from those in operation during the eighth and ninth FYP.(7)

Very roughly the pre-1965 bonus function could have been described by: (the symbols have their usual meaning)

$$B = A + b [Q - Q_p]$$

with A and b being fixed coefficients. The obvious disadvantage of that particular formula was that it encouraged overfulfilment and thus encouraged the hiding of capacity from the planners. The post-1965 approach was by comparison:

$$B = \alpha Q_p + K [Q - Q_p]$$

with $0 < K < 1$ if $Q > Q_p$ and $K > 1$ if $Q_p > Q$

thus encouraging the enterprise to put forward high plans but discouraging overfulfilment.

The bonus formula used for the ninth FYP (1975-79) introduced two significant changes in incentives design that hold true for the schemes used for the tenth and eleventh FYPs. Firstly, the overall size of the planned MIF was linked to a fixed five-year target. This did not necessarily eliminate the ratchet effect but at least it introduced a degree of stability and encouraged the enterprises to plan on more than just a year-to-year basis. Secondly, the size of the MIF and therefore of bonuses received would also depend on the counter-plans, if any, put forward by enterprises.

Initially a great deal of attention was drawn by the planners to the stability of the targets and coefficients of deductions. As we have already seen however in Chapter 4, Soviet planners continue with the practice of changing the annual plans handed to enterprises. Indeed the success of any scheme may well depend on being able to be used flexibly in order to ensure that failures to fulfil the plan are hidden. Another aspect of instability is the tendency of the planners to change basic elements of the bonus system itself in mid course. So for example, within the first year of the tenth FYP, the basis on which the planned MIF was calculated changed from that of the Wage Fund of the base year to the size of the planned MIF for 1975 (i.e. the last year of the preceding, ninth FYP). The reason for this change was to ensure that the MIF did not just grow because the wage fund did. Although this was a reasonable adjustment it nonetheless changed the basis of the calculation of what was meant to be a stable norm for the next five years.

The problem with the dynamic aspects of incentive systems is also likely to remain with the current one. Although the enterprises are now encouraged to put forward higher counter-plans that they should fulfil exactly, there is nothing in the scheme to reward or to counter the disutility of potentially higher future five-year plans. In other words the horizon for the managers is now set on a five-year basis with no guarantees for the next five-year plan.

The bonus system discussed so far stressed the effects of performance over time, and also showed that the ratchet effect of planning from the achieved level might have now moved from an annual to a quinquennial basis. The length of tenure of directors is therefore an important parameter to be accounted for in examining enterprise behaviour and the bonus system. If the managers of the enterprise have either very short tenures at any single establishment or there are available to them wide openings for promotion either horizontally to other enterprises and sectors or vertically in the economic and political command structure, then one could doubt the efficacy of the incentives system to encourage long-term bonus maximisation. Admittedly promotion or demotion may well depend on performance judged on the basis of plan fulfilment but not necessarily on how much money the director earned for him/herself and the rest of the managers and white collar staff.

The evidence from Soviet data is quite intriguing and illuminating.(8) Managerial mobility in the Soviet Union can be considered under two separate headings:

Firstly, the length of tenure at a particular post, here director, in the same enterprise. Secondly, opportunities for promotion outside the enterprise; this could involve horizontal

moves to other enterprises or vertical ones, usually to a ministerial department. Taking length of tenure first, the data
in Tables 6.1 and 6.2 show the remarkable changes that occurred
pre- and post-war.

TABLE 6.1   Mobility of Soviet top executives in heavy industry
in 1934 and 1936 (% of sample)

	Enterprise Directors	First Assistant to Ent. Dir.	Head of Dprts of Entps.
A. Number of years of service in the specific industry			
(i) Less than 5	37	16	No data
(ii) 5 to 10	39	36	"
(iii) More than 10	24	48	"
B. Number of years in same post			
(i) Less than 1	25–34	19–28	22–25
(ii) 1 to 3	40–56	44–64	46–53
(iii) 3 to 5	16–20	13–21	16–18
(iv) More than 5	3– 8	4– 9	6– 4

Source: Granick, Managerial Comparisons ..., p.236. The sample
size for each individual column is given as 457-944,
240-670, 267-343. The source does not explain the
spread of the sample but it is likely that the first
figure refers to 1934 and the other to 1936.

The data in Table 6.1 indicate that more than 75% of enterprise
directors had less than ten years' service in that specific industry and only 3% to 8% of them had more than five years in
the same post. Roughly similar results held for the other two
subordinate posts.

Since the war however the position changed dramatically as
Table 6.2 shows. Although the data in Table 6.2 do not necessarily refer to same industries, or of course to same enterprises as those for Table 6.1, they were drawn from 170 of the
biggest industrial enterprises in the Soviet Union.   So for
example whereas in 1934-36 only 3% to 8% of the directors pol-
led would have held the same post for more than five years that

TABLE 6.2   Continuity in office of enterprise directors
            (% of sample)

Years	January 1953	Average January 1962 and January 1967
Less than 3	57	30
3 to 5	11	18
5 to 10	-	29
Over 10	-	23
Over 5 years	32	52

Source: Granick, Managerial Comparisons ..., p.239

percentage increased to 32 and then to 52 between 1953 and 1967.
It is true that the data in Table 6.1 do not specify whether the
directors held the same post at the same enterprise whereas the
data in Table 6.2 do indicate this. Granick goes on to elaborate
this apparent lengthening in tenure and also to give additional
details of promotion opportunities.

> The lengthening of tenure appears to have been a general
> phenomenon in Soviet society ... A Soviet study of more
> than two hundred junior and middle executives over the age
> of thirty in a large factory in the mid-1960s, showed that
> only 45% had been in their post for less than five years
> and that 29% had held the same position for more than ten
> years. This was despite the fact that 10% of these man-
> agers were under the age of forty ... Furthermore a study
> carried out in the spring of 1965 of personnel in seven
> metal-fabricating enterprises in Leningrad showed that the
> average age of all managers above the foreman level was
> forty-two years. Only 10% of these managers were under
> the age of twenty-five and 75% were twenty-five years or
> older. The authors of this study drew the conclusion that
> one of the main criteria for appointment to a managerial
> position is age and length of service, and stated that
> this conclusion is supported by other data relating to the
> Soviet industry as a whole ... Even in the case of clear
> failure to perform successfully as an enterprise director,
> demotion would not normally occur until the executive held
> his post for four or five years ...
> ... Movement between plans and headquarter organizations
> is also quite limited. Junior executives may start work
> in the ministries or their subdivisions, but it is rare
> for them to be willing to move out to the plants. Plant

executives do indeed move up the headquarter's organizations, but such a move normally occurs after the age of
forty and is a once-and-for-all career development.   At
the same time, the top men of the ministries and their
subdivisions almost always are promoted from the plants
of the same industry.
> (Managerial Comparisons ..., pp.238-39 and 240)

For the Soviet director there are now three possibilities
outside his own enterprise (other than demotion).   Firstly, a
move to the relevant ministry. The vast majority of industrial
ministers have worked as directors in one or more enterprise of
their ministries. The post in the ministry however must be
commensurate to the status and salary of the enterprise director
and therefore the possibilities are very limited.   Secondly,
a transfer 'sideways' as the director of a larger enterprise.
In promotions however, there seem to be preference for existing
members of the enterprise. Thirdly, exit from industrial management into a political-managerial post with the local Communist party organisation. Granick points out that this appears
to be an unusual career change. He summarised the overall position thus

> ... Soviet careers of the middle 1930s were highly mobile
> and apparently included a good deal of movement in both
> directions between enterprises and higher organizations.
> By the 1960s, to the contrary, tenure in posts throughout
> industry had become extremely lengthy and shifting from
> ministerial headquarters to enterprises had become rare.
> Promotional opportunities were scarce, and the position of
> factory director was normally a terminal one.
> (Granick, Managerial Comparisons ..., p.245)

The relevance of all this material to the bonus structure
is obvious. In the post-war period directorial-managerial tenure was stabilised and became increasingly lengthy.   Not only
promotion opportunities became scarcer but movements between
enterprises less easy. Managers now associate their careers
with one enterprise. This may have a positive result in the
sense that as the individual time horizon lengthened, directors
might have slowly changed towards becoming long rather than
short term bonus maximisers. Whether this however did happen is
still a very open question especially in view of the frequency
of changes in the plans and in the bonus system itself.

6.3 OTHER PREMIA AND BONUSES

In addition to the premia paid from the MIF and the wages fund
for the fulfilment of planned targets, workers, and ITR may receive additional premia from the following five sources.   The

148

Incentive Funds and Bonuses

funds for these premia come mainly from MIF but the rules and
conditions for paying them are different from those governing
the premia for the fulfilment of the main planned targets. Furthermore the conditions for the payments of these bonuses may
not depend directly on planned targets per se.   This differ-
entiates them from the bonuses payable from MIF which were discussed in Section 6.2 above.

Firstly, the annual bonus fund.   This is paid out of the
MIF to both ITR and workers. The premia are expressed as a percentage of the annual average earnings of each class of workers.
What constitutes average yearly earnings varies a great deal
from industry to industry. In certain cases in addition to the
actual wages or salaries received, earnings may include premia
and bonuses already received from MIF and the wages fund under
other incentive schemes. The actual amount received depends on
the continuous annual length of service of the persons concerned.
So one aim of this scheme is to discourage labour turnover and
induce a continuity in the production team.   The bonuses are
payable on the condition that planned targets such as profitability have been fulfilled. In the cases of under-fulfilment the
bonus is reduced by an equivalent percentage of the fall in the
size of the MIF resulting from the under-fulfilment of the
planned targets.(9) Table 6.3 gives an example of the scales
applicable to a factory in Odessa.

TABLE 6.3   Scale of payments of annual bonus as a percentage
of average yearly wages and salaries for the personnel of an agricultural machinery plan in Odessa,
1971

Length of service in years	Piece rate workers	Hourly rate workers	ITR	Salaried
1 - 3 (Basic Depts)	3.7	5.0	5.0	5.4
2 - 3 (Auxiliary Depts)	3.7	5.0	5.0	5.4
3 - 5	4.1	5.4	5.4	5.8
5 - 10	4.5	6.2	5.8	6.2
10 - 15	5.0	6.6	6.6	7.0
Over 15	5.4	7.9	7.0	7.5

Source: V.A. Stokolos, Povyshenie effektivnosti premirovaniya
ITR v promyshlennosti, Moscow 1974, p.79.

Secondly, the fund for the introduction and assimilation of new techniques and technology. This fund is formed from the cost savings of the new techniques. Enterprises are instructed to deduct a certain percentage of the factory cost of goods produced with the new techniques (usually 0.3% to 3%) which is then appropriated by the relevant Ministry. From this central fund payments are then made to enterprises using or introducing new and improved techniques of production. There is a fixed scale setting out the amount of cost reductions that can be paid into the fund. For example, for cost savings or improved efficiency resulting in cost reductions up to 10,000 roubles, then 6% to 25% of the savings may be paid into the fund up to a ceiling of 2,000 roubles. For 10,000 to 20,000 roubles savings the relevant figures are 5% to 20% and 3,400 roubles and so on, to 5 million roubles and over where the norms are 0.5% to 3% with a ceiling of 200,000 roubles.(10) The distribution of the total sums collected to the organisations and enterprises depends on the degree of complexity of the task undertaken. For example 30% to 50% of the fund might be allocated to enterprises which were involved in the utilisation and application of scientific work, 20% to 35% to those further developing and elaborating technology and so on.

Thirdly, the fund for the production of high quality goods for domestic consumption or export. The fund is formed out of the profits made from the sale of these goods. Limits are set both as to the duration of the payments of premia (usually the first year of the introduction of the goods) and the percentage of profits paid out.(11)

Fourthly, premia for interfactory and interplant socialist competition. The fund is set up on the basis of comparisons of the degree of fulfilment of planned tasks of factories, plants or brigades of workers. The fund is formed from the MIF from the profits generated by fulfilling these tasks. The norms used vary from Ministry to Ministry. The actual premia are expressed as a percentage of the wages fund, but in general cannot exceed 50% of the monthly wage of any single recipient.(12) The allocation of these funds amongst workers and ITR for the whole industrial sector during 1974-76 is given in Table 6.4. It is interesting to note the larger amounts receivable by ITR.

TABLE 6.4   Premia for socialist competition in industry
(rubles per person per annum)

1974		1975		1976	
Worker	ITR	Worker	ITR	Worker	ITR
7.2	12	8.3	13	9.1	15

Source: A.I. Milyukov: Khozraschetnoe stimulirovanie, Moscow 1979, pp.177-78.

Incentive Funds and Bonuses

Fifthly, the fund for the saving of energy, heat and electricity and for the saving and use of scrap metals (ferrous or non-ferrous, and precious metals). The premia are paid out either from the costs saved or from the value of the scrap metals surrendered or used. In the case of energy savings the premia cannot exceed 75% of the monthly wages at any quarter. The payment of these premia are not dependent on the fulfilment of other planned targets, unless the enterprise was given a specific plan for energy saving or scrap utilisation.(13)

6.4 BONUSES AND INCOMES

The question of the importance of these premia is a relative one because of the impossibility of defining what constitutes a 'substantial proportion of pay' derived from premia and bonuses. In addition to this, some of the statistical sources quote premia as percentages of wage rates or of the total wage or salary fund as opposed to the more relevant average monthly or yearly earnings. The available figures, however, reveal a significant pattern over the short time that these schemes have been in operation, especially in the post-1970 period by which time most industrial enterprises were working under the 1965 reform regulations. Not surprisingly ITR and managers were receiving by the mid-1970s more than a fifth of their average wages in the form of bonuses. This is confirmed by the data in Tables 6.5 and 6.6.

TABLE 6.5   Bonuses in industry as percentage of average wages in 1960-73

	1960	1965	1966	1967	1968	1969	1970	1973
All employees	6.6	8.7	10.3	11.7	12.9	14.4	15.4	16.3
Manual workers	6.0	8.0	9.2	10.2	11.4	12.9	13.8	15.2
ITR including managers	11.0	13.7	16.6	19.2	20.5	21.9	23.6	22.1
Administrative staff	4.6	7.2	12.4	14.4	16.8	18.3	20.1	-

Source: Quoted in Adam, The Present Soviet Incentive Systems p.360. Adams points out that as the data refer to all bonuses, those for manual workers will include bonuses paid out of the wage fund as well as the MIF.

TABLE 6.6   The share of premia in the average wage of
industrial workers in 1973 (%)

	Total	From MIF
Industrial-productive personnel	16.3	8.1
Workers	15.2	5.0
ITR	22.1	22.1

Source: Yu. Artemov, Ekonomicheskie granitsi fonda material'-
nogo pooshchreniya, Voprosy Ekonomiki, No.8 1975, p.40.

TABLE 6.7   Bonuses as a percentage of salary

	All employed	ITR
All bonuses and awards of which:	16.8	28.0
(a) Bonuses from Wage Fund	8.4	2.7
(b) Bonuses from the general bonus fund	6.8	20.7
(c) All other bonuses of which:	1.6	4.6
(i) Innovation Bonus Fund	0.34	na
(ii) Export bonus	0.27	na
(iii) Socialist competition prizes	0.19	na
(iv) Producing consumer goods from waste	0.13	na
(v) Economising on fuels	0.11	na

Source: Vasil'ev and Chistiakova, Effektivnost' oplaty
upravlencheskogo truda v promyshlenosti, Moscow 1972,
pp.99 and 124, quoted in Berliner, The Innovation
Decision ..., p.480. No date is given for the data.
The general bonus fund is the MIF. The source does
not specify whether the data refer to the whole industrial sector or a sample of it. Berliner points
out that some personnel although classified as ITR,
apparently receive bonuses from the wage fund.

Incentive Funds and Bonuses

The data of Table 6.7 reconfirm the impressions gained
from Tables 6.5 and 6.6, but taken in conjunction with those of
Table 6.8, lead to a number of interesting observations.
Firstly, ITR and managers receive the greatest share of the MIF.
This is not surprising as the MIF is the primary source of bonuses for them, whereas workers may receive premia from the wage
fund as well. It now follows that the single most important
use of the MIF is to provide a substantial proportion of the
income of ITR and managers. With the exception of the annual
bonus, the proportion of MIF directed to other funds and premia
is very small and in any case these other bonuses account for a
very small percentage of wages of workers. Even in the case of
the annual bonus which in the early 1970s accounted for about
40% of the use of the MIF for all industry, it apparently
generated, for a sample of enterprises, less than 5.5% of the
yearly wages in terms of bonuses.(14)

TABLE 6.8   Allocation of MIF (in %) amongst different workers
and for different purposes in a sample of 549
industrial enterprises

	1966	1967	1968	1969	1970	1971	1972 (planned)
Current premia to							
Workers	10.5	14.4	21.2	17.6	17.3	17.3	18.3
ITR	46.7	34.0	27.4	25.5	25.8	26.1	28.4
Salaried	6.8	6.0	4.6	4.4	4.4	4.3	4.6
Annual bonus	14.8	26.8	30.7	32.0	30.6	31.1	31.1
Extra premia	10.7	10.7	9.0	7.9	7.3	6.3	4.8
Socialist com- petition premia	2.0	2.0	2.0	2.2	2.6	3.1	3.3
Material help to individuals	8.5	6.1	5.1	5.0	4.9	5.1	4.8
To socio- cultural and Housing Fund	–	–	–	3.5	5.0	4.7	2.6
Other purposes	–	–	–	1.9	2.1	1.9	2.1

Source: Milyukov, Pooshchritel'nie fondy na predpriyatii,
Moscow 1974, p.149.

153

Finally, two further sets of data in Tables 6.9 and 6.10 reconfirm the relative unimportance of MIF as a source of income for industrial workers and those that work in the supply system. Although the Gossnab data in Table 6.9 are not strictly speaking directly relevant as they do not refer to industrial enterprises, they are interesting in that they provide a parallel confirmation of the developments in the industrial sector.

TABLE 6.9   Premia paid to Gossnab USSR personnel expressed as a percentage of the total wage fund for each category of workers (S = salaried, W = workers).

	General Premia		Annual Bonus		Extra Premia for Special Tasks		Premia from Wages Fund (Workers only)
	ITR & S	W	ITR & S	W	ITR & S	W	
1974	18.0	2.4	4.1	2.2	0.6	0.4	12.0
1975	17.6	2.5	4.1	2.2	0.6	0.3	12.5

Source: Kurotchenko & Gyurman, Ekonomicheskoe stimulirovanie ..., pp.206-7

It is clearly apparent that there is a veritable dearth of recent, systematic and consistently calculated data on the percentage that premia and bonuses account for salaries and wages. Adam, referring to the data in Table 6.5, observed:

> To our knowledge there are no accessible figures on the extent of differentiation within the indicated aggregate data. It would be interesting to know what the share of top managers is in the bonus fund. What we have are figures - thanks to a Gosbank inquiry in 1974 - on the share of bonuses (from all sources) in earnings. According to these 23.5% of top managers received bonuses amounting to 38-50% of earnings, 48.8% of top managers received 51-60% and 16.3% received 65%. For the remaining 11.4% of top managers who certainly received above 65%, no figures are indicated.
> (The Present Soviet Incentive System, p.360)

The Gosbank findings referred to above offer a tantalising glimpse into the potential importance of bonuses for managerial incomes and therefore motivation.

The conclusions from this admittedly fragmented evidence is

TABLE 6.10 Structure of earnings from different sources for industrial workers (% of total)

	Payments according to tariff rates			Payments for overfulfilling production norms	Premia				Other*
	Total	Piece rates	Time rates		Total	From wage fund; piece workers	From wage fund; time workers	From MIF	
1961	75.2	46.9	28.3	Not available	7.1	3.3	3.8	Not available	17.7 }**
1972	67.1	42.7	24.4	Not available	15.3	5.2	5.1	5.0	17.6
1973-74	72.5	40.5	32.0	7.6	13.6	6.3	5.0	2.3	6.3

Source: Kynel'ski, Povyshenie stimuliruyushchei ...., pp.61 and 77.

* End of year bonuses, regional premia etc.
The data for 1973-74 are apparently provisional. Increases in the tariff rates and the growing role of MIF since 1972 make meaningful comparisons difficult between the years.

** The payments for overfulfilling norms are usually considered part of the overall pay structure. If in 1961 and 1972 these payments were not significantly different from 1973-74 this will reduce the discrepancy in the last column for the 1961-1972 and the 1973-74 data.

155

obvious. Bonuses and premia, especially those deriving from
the MIF are quantitatively far more important for the managers
and ITR than for the workers. The incentive schemes centred
around the MIF are therefore primarily designed to motivate managers than workers. The rest of the bonus system and other
premia do not appear either to be of significant quantitative
importance for workers. One could therefore doubt their operational and practical significance.

6.5 EVIDENCE ON THE EFFECTIVENESS OF BONUSES

An alternative way of exploring the potential influence of the
MIF and the rest of the incentive scheme is to examine the degree of relationship between the size or the changes of the MIF
and the index which determine its size.

Three recent studies have done just that but with conflicting and ambiguous results.(15)

The first study to be examined here by Drize was effectively a simulation exercise as it regressed the planned level of
MIF against the planned levels of fund-forming indexes such as
output, profits etc. for 1971-75. The study is therefore of
limited value as it shows the relationships, if any, of these
variables at a planned stage only rather than the actual outcome.
Even so the results are interesting because they highlight the
difficulties of coordinating the growth of MIF at the planning
stage with that of the key target variables.

The Drize study used four linear and log linear models re-
gressing either the absolute planned level of MIF (Y) or changes
in it against either the absolute level or percentage changes in
the levels of the planned annual sales (X_1) level of profitability (X_2), labour and productivity (X_3) and wages fund (X_4).
Annual data from 35 machine tool and engineering enterprises
were used spanning the 1971-75 period.(16) No regression coefficients are given, but the model with the highest $R^2 = 0.69$,
was linear using absolute values. All the coefficients were
statistically significant at the 1,98 t-level except for the
wages fund.

The partial correlation coefficients for the linear model
were as follows:

$$YX_1 = 0.58, \quad YX_2 = 0.27, \quad YX_3 = 0.17, \quad YX_4 = 0.05$$

The cross-correlation coefficients were in general higher for
the linear models using absolute levels. The MIF, wages fund,
and labour productivity had cross correlation coefficients in
the 0.60s which is not surprising given that wages and productivity tend to move together and that the MIF is expressed as a
percentage of the wages fund.

The Kletskii study undertook a similar exercise but with
actual as opposed to planned data spanning 1970-73 for 35 machine
building enterprises in Byelorussia.(17) The text is not clear

Incentive Funds and Bonuses

as to the form of the data used but it is most likely that indexes for the MIF (Y) were regressed against indexes for the actual level of output (X_1), gross profit (X_2), labour productivity (X_3), the proportion of salaries of ITR and salaried personnel to the total wages fund (X_4), and the wage fund itself (X_5). As a variation, similar equations were run but instead of gross profit X_2, gross profitability X_2^* was used.

For the first type of regression the R^2 obtained were as follows:

1970 0.68,   1971 0.002,   1972 0.31,   1973 0.30

For the second type:

1970 0.67,   1971 0.02,   1972 0.32,   1973 0.35

A typical set of equations (exluding 1971 which generally produced a poor fit) is reproduced below.

1970 $Y = -315.7 + 2.81(X_1) + 0.2(X_2) + 0.24(X_3) - 1.15(X_4)$

$- 1.58(X_5)$ with $R^2 = 0.68$

1972 $Y = 0.55 + 0.49(X_1) + 0.4(X_2) + 0.08(X_3) + 0.39(X_4)$

$+ 0.11(X_5)$ with $R^2 = 0.31$

1970 $Y = -365.3 + 2.71(X_1) + 0.07(X_2^*) + 0.43(X_3) - 0.86(X_4)$

$- 1.52(X_5)$ with $R^2 = 0.67$

1973 $Y = -207.13 + 0.79(X_1) + 0.25(X_2^*) + 0.935(X_3) + 0.07(X_4)$

$+ 0.087(X_5)$ with $R^2 = 0.35$

The author however adds as an afterthought that none of all the coefficients was statistically significant for the t-test!

These results taken in conjunction with those found in the Drize study are indeed surprising. There appears to be either a weak or no relationship at all between the MIF and the indexes used for its formation either on an ex ante (planned) or on an ex post basis. The form of the relationship (linear or log linear or in terms of changes of the variables) does not appear to affect the results in the sense that even the best equations produce relatively small R^2. Kletskii even claims that non linear functions were unlikely to produce better results.

The Vasil'eva study used actual as opposed to planned data from 80 light and food industry enterprises in the RSFSR spanning the years 1966-74. The following four linear regression models were tested for each year (models 1 to 4 respectively)

157

$$X_4 \text{ or } X_5 \text{ or } X_6 \text{ or } X_7 \text{ as} = f(X_1 \, X_2 \, X_3)$$

where X_1 = rate of growth of sales, X_2 = rate of growth of labour productivity, X_3 = level of profitability, X_4 = MIF in roubles, X_5 = rate of growth of MIF, X_6 = MIF/wages, X_7 = MIF/ workers.

The results of the regression were as follows:

For model 1 for years 1966-70 the author does not give R^2 or t-test results, but the F test was significant only in 1967. So irrespective of the size of R^2 the equations did not produce a reliable fit. Indeed for 1966 and 1969 the coefficients of X_1 were negative - a highly unlikely result. For the same time period, using model 2 produced F tests that were significant only for 1969 and 1970. Similar poor results were obtained by models 3 and 4. It would appear that during the eighth FYP there was no discernible statistical link between MIF (in absolute or growth terms) and all the relevant fund-forming indexes.

A series of tests using the available data for the ninth FYP produced poor partial correlation coefficients. Model 1 was not significant for the whole period. Models 2 to 4 produced poor results for 1973 and 1974 but for 1971 and 1972 growth of sales and labour productivity explained little more than 20% of the movements of MIF.

Kletskii and Vesil'eva offered the following explanation for the failure to detect any significant statistical relationship between the MIF and the key targets.

Kletskii claims that as his data span two FYPs (the eighth and the ninth) the changes in planned targets and in the incentives system after 1972 might have disrupted the relationship. There were problems with 'correcting' the MIF in cases where there were wide discrepancies between actual and planned targets. Finally the system of price formation and the allocation of investment resources led to fluctuations in the profitability of enterprises over time.

Vasil'eva suggested three explanations for the poor fit of her data.

Firstly, those enterprises transferred to the new economic system after 1965 received high targets and also higher allocation of MIF but the growth rate of output, profit etc. fell because they exhausted quickly their productive reserves. Secondly, 1967, 1968 and 1973 were years in which price changes affected both the value of output and profitability. The poor harvest of 1972 also affected theoutput of the food industries in the sample. Thirdly, until 1968 profitability depended only on the size of profits as the cost of capital was constant. From 1968 the cost of capital increased faster than profits, especially for enterprises that were re-equipping their plants.

A slightly different but more generalised explanation of these particular findings can be attempted along the following lines. Strictly speaking the size of the MIF depends proportionally on the size of the wage fund (for those years where its planned size was expressed as a percentage of the wage fund) and the degree of fulfilment of planned targets. There are two cases under which this relationship might break down: firstly, if the increases in the actual performance falls well short of the planned targets, in which case the MIF will either remain relatively constant or decline. Secondly, if the authorities change either the norms used to form the fund, keeping the plans constant, or change the plans and the norms simultaneously so that the expected relationship between MIF and these indexes breaks down. The MIF may then vary independently of the size of the variables which are supposed to determine it. Given that the annual plans of enterprises are subject to frequent changes (especially if that will ensure fulfilment or overfulfilment, see pp.109-11 in this book) it is not surprising that the correlation of the MIF with targets is weak. In addition to this the behaviour of the MIF over time, or amongst enterprises, is likely to be affected not so much by the absolute level of the variables which determine it, but by the relationship between the planned and the actual targets. After all, incentive schemes tend to encourage exact fulfilment and the 'ratchet effect' tends to discourage overfulfilment. This effect was intensified with the post-1972 MIF rules which penalised, in relative terms, overfulfilment.

The Drize study attempted to explore the possibility that there was a systematic pattern of relationship between the annual enterprise plans and those prescribed in the FYP (1971-75) and the size of the MIF. The data used for the comparison were the FYP magnitudes sent down to the enterprises and the confirmed annual plans that enterprises were finally expected to carry out.

From the sample of the 35 enterprises, 26 were classified into five groups in the following manner: (the source does not give the number of each groups)

(a) Those enterprises whose annual 'fund-forming indexes' did not deviate much from those set out and prescribed in their FYPS.
(b) Those whose annual indexes did deviate most during the first two years of the FYP.
(c) Those whose annual indexes did deviate most during the next two years of the FYP.
(d) Those whose annual indexes deviated throughout the FYP.
(e) And finally, those whose rate of growth of output fluctuated in relation to that prescribed in the FYP but whose growth of profitability and productivity remained unchanged in relation to the FYP targets.

The lowest R^2 was 0.68 and the highest 0.73. The partial correlation coefficients for all five groups were roughly similar. All the coefficients were statistically significant. Partial correlation coefficients between MIF and the level of sales,

profitability and labour productivity and overall R^2 were obtained for all the five groups. To the extent that deviations
from the FYP reflected the degree by which enterprises could
bargain with the Gosplan for tighter or looser annual plans,
then the correlation between MIF and the planned targets was not
affected irrespective of the actual years in which the deviation,
if any, occurred. Furthermore, it was observed that for two
specific years, 1971 and 1972, if the annual fund-forming indexes deviated by 1% from the FYP annual targets in 1971, then
the correlation coefficient between the indexes and MIF was
0.27 and the partial correlation coefficients for output, profitability and labour productivity were 0.08, 0.22 and 0.23. In
1972 with the deviation increasing to 5% the coefficients increased to 0.61 and 0.21, 0.26 and 0.5 respectively.

It appeared that there was a correlation between the wid-
ening of the divergence of the annual and the FYP targets and
the degree by which the MIF was linked to these targets. Higher
correlation between planned targets and planned MIF did not
imply a higher absolute MIF for the enterprise, but at least it
indicated a systematic relationship between the two as the deviation increased. This was of considerable importance to Drize's
study which laid great emphasis on the benefits to enterprises
in terms of higher bonuses in seeking and accepting higher annual plans compared to the FYP targets.

Some evidence collected by Drize on actual as opposed to
planned performance was not encouraging however. From a sample
of 75 enterprises in the machine tool, metallurgical, light,
and food processing industries, 51 (i.e. more than 60%) had
overfulfilled their sales (output) plan for 1972. This sample
included enterprises that had received lower or higher annual
plans for 1972 compared to their FYP plans. Apparently there
was no systematic relationship between overfulfilment and rec-
ceiving a relatively loose or tight plan. At the same time
however there was virtually no difference between the size of
the planned MIF expressed as a percentage of the wages fund between enterprises that had overfulfilled the targets set by the
FYP and those enterprises that had received 'relatively taut
plans'. By implication this meant enterprises which received
higher annual plans compared to the FYP targets. In fact the
latter group ended up with a planned MIF smaller than that of
the former. Although the source does not indicate the final
actual size of MIF the conclusion was that the incentives system
did not appear to encourage enterprises to suggest higher
annual plans.

6.6 CONCLUSIONS

The econometric evidence on the link between fund-forming indexes and MIF is apparently very weak. This might not be surprising in view of the frequent changes in both the bonus schemes

and plans during the time period covered by the three studies summarised above. In addition to this there is the problem of the quality of the data and the fact that there is no theory being tested here. Strictly speaking MIF and the fund-forming indexes should bear some proportional relationship to each other and hence produce a very close statistical fit. The fact that they did not may be the result of a non-linear relationship or the constant plan changes that ensured that MIF grew irrespective of the performance of the enterprise. The statistical results should raise some serious doubts as to the efficacy of the material incentives system in influencing enterprise behaviour if only rewards but no penalties are meted out by the planners.

It is interesting to note however that the Drize study has produced some evidence as to how the plan itself might affect decisions, in the sense that as the annual plans diverged from the overall FYP the correlation between planned MIF and the planned indexes increased. There was however no systematic evidence that the highest correlation between MIF and the indexes occurred when there was no divergence at all between annual and FY plans. If that had been the case, then it could have been argued that this was evidence that taut planning, in the sense of encouraging enterprises to accept higher annual plans without any additional allocation of inputs, produce close movements in targets and planned MIF, or conversely that when MIF and targets were highly correlated enterprises were producing close to the capacity they had chosen to reveal to planners.

As none of the studies available contained data on the correlation between actual MIF received and the differences between annual counter plan and actual performance, the relationship between tautness and bonuses still remains an open question.

Finally the statistical evidence shows clearly that the incentive schemes are directed towards influencing managerial staff and the large number of additional bonus schemes and premia appear to be so small as a percentage of earnings as to cast doubts on their relevance to decision-making. The lengthening of the tenure of enterprise managers might be a desirable development in fostering continuity and stability. In view however of the lack of any reliable evidence on the relationship between MIF, counter-plans and actual performance, the lengthening of tenure on its own is hardly likely to throw any light on managerial motivation or begin to produce some evidence on whether Soviet managers are long-term bonus maximisers.

Incentive Funds and Bonuses

Notes

1.   Since we are concerned here with individual bonus
payments we shall disregard the Socio-cultural and Housing
Fund and the Development of Production Fund which do not affect
directly the take-home pay of workers and managers.   The rules
described here apply equally to single enterprises as well   as
to associations.

2.   A.E. Kunel'skii in Povyshenie stimuliruyushchei   roli
zarabotnoi platy i optimizatsiya ee struktury, Moscow 1975,
gives details of productivity bonuses paid in addition to wages
at the Volzhskom car factory. For example for 90-90% fulfilment
of production norms, 1% of the basic wage rate was paid as   a
bonus, for 91-91% fulfilment 2% and for 96-100 - 4%.   For increases in productivity and labour efficiency a minimum of 10%
to a maximum of 20% of the wage rate could be paid (pp.163-65).
Another example is quoted in the Ekonomicheskaya Gazeta, No.7,
Feb.1979, pp.11-14 for the Avtovaz light car plant. Payments to
workers consist of three parts. Firstly the time rate which is
sub-divided into three components; (a) the standard hourly rate,
(b) additional payments as a percentage of the hourly rate for
monotonous, intensive or heavy work, (c) ditto for production
of goods without defects etc. Secondly, payments for fulfilling
the work norms, again expressed as a percentage of the hourly
rate. Thirdly, premia for the reduction of 'labour intensity'
of the work carried out.

3.   This section draws heavily from the 'osnovye polozheniya' on the formation of MIF for the eleventh FYP published
in Ekonomicheskaya Gazeta Nos.15 and 17, April 1980. See also
general discussion in A. Akhmednev, 'Fond material'nogo pooshchreniya', Voprosy Ekonomiki No.6, 1981, pp.41-49; Yu. M.
Armenov, 'Fondy pooshchreniya v odinnadtsatoi pyatiletke', in
Finansii SSSR, No.10, 1980, pp.12-17.   The rules concerning
the formation of MIF for the eleventh FYP are basically the
same for those of the tenth FYP (1976-1980). The rules concerning
the tenth FYP can be found in Fondy Pooshchreniya obyedinenii i
predpriyatii v desyatoi pyatiletke (osnovye polozheniya)   in
Ekonomicheskaya Gazeta, No.50, Dec. 1976; Fondy pooshchreniya
predpriyatii mestnoi promyshlennosti, Ekonomicheskaya Gazeta No.
18, April 1977; V.P. Ignatushkin, Fondy pooshchreniya v desyatoi pyatiletke in Finansii SSSR, No.3, 1977, pp.73-80.

For an extensive discussion of incentives schemes in the
Soviet Union see J. Adam, 'The Present Soviet Incentive System'
in Soviet Studies Vol.32, No.3, July 1980, pp.349-65. Some of
the material appearing in this chapter (especially in Sections
6.4 and 6.5) draws from A.F. Freris, The Quantitative Importance
of Incentives Funds and Bonuses in Soviet Industrial Enterprises:
Some Recent Empirical Evidence in F.L. Altman (Ed.), Year Book
of East European Economics, Band 9/II, Gunter Olzog Verlag,
Munich 1981, pp.185-205.

4.   For some indirect and rather vague references, see

Ekonomicheskaya Gazeta No.23, June 1975, p.14, Pooshchritel'nye fondy na 1976 god, and Ekonomicheskaya Gazeta No.15, April 1977, Fondi pooshchrenya slyzby byta v decyatoi pyatiletke. In the latter reference a comment is made to the effect that the establishment of the planned MIF must take into account the performance and targets of the enterprises concerned.

5.   For rules concerning the distribution of MIF amongst the managers and workers during the eleventh FYP see Ekonomicheskaya Gazeta No.39, 1980.

6.   The engineering technical workers include all the shopfloor administrative/technical personnel such as chief technician, quality controllers etc.   To these another group is usually added, salaried personnel, which include all the office workers, accountants and book-keepers, secretaries etc. To void repetition the ITR-salaried distinction is made only where Soviet sources indicate a clear differentiation.   It is important however to note that ITR is also generally taken to include the director and section managers of an enterprise. Again where necessary a distinction will be made between managers and ITR.   See I.P. Kovalkii, Spravochnik po uchetu truda i zarabotnoi platy, Moscow 1977, pp.9-11.

7.   The following discussion is based primarily on M. Loeb and W.A. Magat, Success Indicators in the Soviet Union: The Problem of Incentives and Efficient Allocations, in American Economic Review Vol.67, No.5, March 1978, pp.173-81.   For the discussion on the pre- and post-1965 schemes see M. Ellman, Soviet Planning Today, Cambridge University Press, Cambridge 1971, Ch.8 passim.

8.   The discussion in the following section draws heavily from D. Granick, Managerial Comparisons in Four Developed Countries: France, Britain, US and Russia, MIT Press, Massachusetts 1972, Ch.8 passim.

9.   Kovalkii,Spravochnik ..., pp.49-50, M.A. Azarkh and A.G. Bondarenko, Povyshenie stimuliruyushchei roli godogo voznagrazhdeniya, Moscow 1977, passim.

10.   P.A. Sedlov, Material'noe stimulirovanie rabotnikov za sozdanie i osvoenie novoi tekhniki, Moscow 1975, pp.6 and 38-39.

11.   I.M. Zavarikhin, Fondy ekonomicheskogo stimulirovanya, Moscow 1976, p.12.

12.   Z.L. Zhitintskii, et al., Sotsialisticheskoe sorevnovanie na promyshlennikh predpriyatiyakh, Moscow 1977, pp.12-42.

13.   Zavarikhin, Fondy ekonomicheskogo ..., p.11; Kovalkii, Spravochnik ..., pp.50-55.

14.   Azarkh and Bondarenko, Povyshenie stimuliruyushchei ..., pp.13 and 36-37, quoting data for eight food processing plants in Moscow and Volgograd.

15.   I.D. Drize and Zh. I. Sidorova, Obrazovanie pooshchritel'nykh fondov na predpriyatiyakh, Moscow 1975, pp.1-63, referred from now on as the Drize study.

Incentive Funds and Bonuses

V.I. Kletskii, Material'noe stimulirovanie proizvodstven-
nikh kollectivov v promyshlenosty, Minsk 1976, pp.211-21, referred to as the Kletskii study.
N.A. Vasil'eva, Fond matelial'nogo pooshchreniya i fondoo-
vrazuyushchie pokazeteli.   In Izvestiya Sibirskogo Otdeleniya
A.N.SSSR, (Seriya obshchestvennykh nauk) No.11, 1977, pp.137-43
referred to as the Vasil'eva study.
16.   The details given in the book of the statistical
techniques used are inadequate.   The text does not make clear
whether cross sectional and time series data are aggregated
together.
17.   A clear distinction was made here between cross section and time series data since separate equations were fitted
for each of the four years examined.   In addition to this the
author tested for multicollinearity by using a matrix of cross
correlation coefficients of the data involved.   Kletskii adds
to the MIF all premia derived from the wages fund as well. One
explanation for this would have been lack of disaggregate data.
Kletskii however presents a table on p.218 with the cross correlation coefficients between MIF and the five planned indexes.
MIF is given here in two forms: including and excluding premia
from the wages fund.   The change in the definition makes very
little difference in the two sets of the cross correlation coefficients.   In view of the poor statistical fit of the
equations with the MIF which includes premia from the wages fund
it is unlikely that the results would change if the MIF definition was altered. Given that the MIF is designed as the source
of bonus almost exclusively for the ITR and the directors it is
all the more puzzling why Kletskii used that definition but did
not offer any explanation for doing this.

Chapter Seven
SUMMARY AND CONCLUSION

The description and analysis of the behaviour of the Soviet enterprise has raised a number of issues that can now be summarised. It must now be apparent that there is no unified or
general theory that will predict and explain the course of action
of the Soviet industrial enterprise. It may well be tempting
to draw a parallelism with the problems faced when modelling
the behaviour of the capitalist firm in an imperfectly competitive market. There are a number of models but no general theory.
It is however important to remember that the theory of the firm
in a market economy boils down to the theory of markets. The
motivation of the firm may well be different, profit or sales
maximisation and so on, but the degree of competition will be
crucial in determining output, prices and profits. The theory
of the Soviet enterprise addresses itself to a different class
of problems as the background against which the enterprise will
operate will not be competitive or uncompetitive markets but its
relations with the planners, with other enterprises and lastly
with consumers. The latter may influence enterprise behaviour
via the feedback that either enterprises pass on to the planners
or by direct observation of the state of individual sectors by
the planners themselves. Hence enterprise behaviour is primarily conditioned by this continuous interaction with the planners.
The institutional and planning framework under which the
Soviet enterprise is operating in the 1980s is still a highly
centralised one. There is every indication that the degree of
centralisation is increasing both in terms of the growing role
of associations and in terms of the concentration of production
in the hands of a smaller number of enterprises and/or associations. An analytical approach to the behaviour of the enterprise must therefore concentrate even further on the role and
games of the planners and the planned and the 'unofficial'
degree of freedom that the enterprises either are allowed to
enjoy or manoeuvre themselves into enjoying. The planning system
may appear rigid but it is totally reliant for its functioning
on information which the lower echelons provide. The planners
can cajole or coerce information out of the planned. Coercion

plays virtually no role now in ensuring performance and fulfilment of tasks. Instead, incentives and bonuses are used or
changes are made in the institutional structure or in the targets handed down or in the 'rules of the game' in order to extract more information from the enterprise and to ensure
greater compliance with the plans. The enterprises do enjoy a
considerable degree of freedom in supplying the centre with the
information necessary for more accurate planning, for example,
by revealing true productive capacities, hidden inventories etc.
Whether the enterprises will do so or not will depend on a combination of factors including the overall pressure exerted on
them and the long-term financial rewards involved in any given
course of action.

An important aspect of the production operations of enterprises involves the Gossnab in its role as the planner of input
allocation and supplies. The Gossnab can be examined as a separate institutional entity in the sense that it has its own
aims, plans, incentive schemes etc.   But in terms of its role
and influence on enterprise behaviour it has to be subsumed
within the Soviet planning framework. Enterprise behaviour is
an integral component of the supply mechanism behaviour because
enterprises reflect in their actions the aims of the supply
planners.

Gossnab does not act as a major inventories holder or
a supplier of goods; these are roles reserved for the enterprises under its auspices. There are reasons to believe that
changes are on the way that may well move the Gossnab towards
becoming a centralised inventories holder. This would be a major
headache for Soviet planners and would take the economy much
further down the road to centralisation than the present rulers
and practical considerations may deem desirable.

The function of the Gossnab as the planner of the flows of
supplies between production units and sectors and that of the
enterprises themselves as the actual suppliers of goods can be
examined more meaningfully within the context of taut planning
and uncertainty.

Monistic models of the enterprise make very limited contributions to the understanding of their behaviour.   Predictions
concerning levels of output in comparison to output or profits
maximising enterprises, factor proportions used, and levels of
costs are interesting but only within a partial equilibrium
framework and are unlikely to be tested, given the paucity of
microeconomic statistical data emanating from the Soviet Union.
The multiproduct model however offers a useful insight into one
aspect of taut planning in terms of input substitution amongst
different goods and the fulfilment of the assortment plan.   An
analysis of more detailed models confirmed the impression that
most of the targets that Soviet enterprises are expected to fulfil may well conflict with each other. Enterprises could respond
from the point of view of Gosplan and Gossnab, in unexpected or
undesirable manner to changes in planned indexes precisely

166

because of these inherent conflicts. The fact that enterprises have some discretion over which targets to fulfil or ignore and the availability of unplanned inputs in the form of hidden reserves, excess capacity, imperfections within the Gossnab system etc, compounded the problems of maintaining control over enterprises.

Increases in the length of managerial tenure may well have encouraged managers to take longer views of the performance of their enterprise, including an attempt at long-term bonus maximisation. At the same time however the practice of changing plans, targets etc. right through the five-year planning period means that despite all promises to the contrary, the plan itself remains uncertain. Furthermore the available empirical evidence shows that plans are frequently changed in order to allow enterprises to fulfil their tasks. Plan fulfilment becomes, so to speak an ex post exercise where apparently plans match performance rather than the other way around. All this does not contribute to 'plan discipline'. It is perhaps ironic that the manager of a planned enterprise lives in an environment as much uncertain as that of his or her capitalist counterpart, although of course the rewards and penalties for facing and taking on these risks and uncertainties are not the same.

Given that the standard neoclassical models of the theory of the firm did not offer much, if any, scope of development in the context of the Soviet industrial enterprise, a number of alternative approaches were tried.

A piecemeal approach taking bonus and tautness considerations together presented a wider and more fruitful scope of analysis.

Tautness, defined generally as the relationship between planned inputs and output, taken together with different bonus schemes produced a number of interesting predictions regarding enterprise behaviour. Actual performance and plans were likely to coincide only regimes of complete certainty. As the complexity of the Soviet economy increased so did the awareness of the planners as to the true magnitude of the tasks that faced them. The quantity and quality of information also increased. Tautness could therefore decrease and the underfulfilment of plans become less frequent, smaller in size or both. The statistical evidence concerning the degree and frequency of underfulfilment in the pre- and post-war periods is not inconsistent with this prediction.

The concept of an optimum level of tautness in plans is a useful analytical device, but on a narrow basis, i.e. on an enterprise level alone. Optimum tautness may help to explain or specify bonus systems that will produce the appropriate level of exhortation, but leaves out of the picture the practicalities of plan consistency on a sectoral or economy-wide level.

Bonus schemes are supposed to deal with the static and dynamic problems facing any incentives system. Bonuses that encouraged overfulfilment allowed an estimate of the true productive

167

capacity of enterprises. Overfulfilment however contained the
seed of the ratchet effect. Bonuses had therefore to compensate
for future higher plans. In the final analysis it was necessary to specify managerial utility functions that incorporated
both the utility of bonuses, disutility of effort and/or the
disutility of higher future plans.

The analysis of different bonus schemes allows predictions
within a probabilistic range of levels of output achieved or
other ratios of actual to planned targets. The statistical
hypotheses involved are far more likely to be useful in explaining past behaviour of enterprises rather than predicting the
future. In addition to this, all the bonus schemes examined involved changes in the coefficients in order to affect the ratios
of actual to planned performance. This is an unrealistic proposition
under the current planning practice in the Soviet Union. Furthermore, the continuing practice of changing planned targets as
well as changing occasionally some of the rules of the incentive
systems themselves during the planned period, reduced or even
nullified the effectiveness of incentives in controlling enterprise behaviour. Dynamic models of the enterprise which included bonus schemes also required precise specification of the
variables involved and could therefore make only limited predictions.

The empirical evidence on the links between incentives'
funds and fund-forming indexes was shown to be very tenuous,
mostly because of imperfections in the data and the techniques
used in the econometric studies and because of the frequent
changes in targets, plans and coefficients that destroyed or
hid any systematic variations or links.

As long as there are no systematic cross-sectional and time
series data on the performance of Soviet enterprises, research
on this area, at least in the west, is likely to remain on theoretical level which frequently verges on pure speculation or on
normative rather than positive approaches to the subject. In
recent years however Soviet authors have started to produce,
with increasing frequency, studies based on micro data which
throw light on previous unknown areas or yield unexpected results. It is very likely that the pursuit of greater efficiency
in the face of a general slowdown in the rate of growth of the
Soviet economy will stimulate further research in the behaviour
and dynamics of the single most important organisational unit
of Soviet industry, the industrial enterprise.

SELECT BIBLIOGRAPHY

This select bibliography contains under broad topic headings a number of important books and articles in English.

Theory of the Socialist Enterprise

E. Ames, Soviet Economic Processes, R.D. Irwin, Illinois 1965, Chs. 3 to 6 inclusive.
T. Buck, Comparative Industrial Systems, Macmillan, London 1982, Ch.3.
I. Jeffries (Ed.), The Industrial Enterprise in Eastern Europe, Praeger, New York 1981.
G.R. Feiwel, The Economics of a Socialist Enterprise, A Case Study of the Polish Firm, Praeger, New York 1965.
D. Granick, Enterprise Guidance in Eastern Europe, Princeton University Press, Princeton 1975.
J.M. Martin, Reforms and the Maximising Behaviour of the Soviet Firm. In J. Thornton (Ed.), Economic Analysis of the Soviet-Type Systems, Cambridge University Press, Cambridge 1977, pp.216-41.

Industrial Planning, Financial Flows and Supplies of Inputs

J.S. Berliner, The Innovation Decision in Soviet Industry, The MIT Press, Massachusetts 1976, Chs. 2 to 6 inclusive.
M. Ellman, Soviet Planning Today, Cambridge University Press, Cambridge 1971, Ch.6.
G. Garvy, Money, Financial Flows and Credit in the Soviet Union, Bollinger, Massachusetts 1977.
A.C. Gorlin, 'The Soviet Economic Associations' Soviet Studies, Vol.26, No.1, January 1977, pp.3-27.
H.S. Levine, 'The Centralised Planning of Supply in Soviet Industry' in Comparisons of US and Soviet Economics, US Government Printing Office, Washington DC, 1959, pp.151-176.
A. Nove, The Soviet Economic System, G. Allen & Unwin, London 1977, Chs. 2 to 4 inclusive.

Select Bibliography

Incentives and Tautness: Theoretical Models

M. Cave and P. Hare,   Alternative Approaches to Economic Planning, Macmillan, London 1981, Ch.9.

S. Gindin,   'A Model of the Soviet Firm', Economics of Planning, Vol.10, No.3, 1970, pp.145-57.

H. Hunter,   'Optimal Tautness in Development Planning' in Economic Development and Cultural Change, Vol.9, July 1961, pp. 561-72.

M. Keren,   'On the Tautness of Plans', Review of Economic Studies, Vol.39, Oct. 1972, pp.469-86.

R.D. Portes,   'The Enterprise Under Central Planning', Review of Economic Studies, Vol.36, April 1969, pp.197-212.

M.L. Weitzman,   'The New Soviet Incentive Model', The Bell Journal of Economics, Vol.7, No.1, Spring 1976, pp.251-57.

See also contributions to a special symposium on the Theory of Incentives reprinted in The Journal of Comparative Economics, Vol.3, No.3, Sept. 1979.

Incentives and Bonuses: Current Practice and Problems

J. Adam,   'The Present Soviet Incentive Systems', Soviet Studies, Vol.32, No.3, July 1980, pp.349-65.

M. Ellman,   Soviet Planning Today, Cambridge University Press, Cambridge 1971, Ch.8.

SUBJECT INDEX

Subject Index

pre- and post-1965 systems
    144-45
inconsistent plans
    corrections for 39
    consequences 45-48
inputs
    planned allocation 37-39
    unplanned availability 93-97
inventories
    and bonus systems 129
    relative size 44-45
    tautness in plans 105

Khozraschet 4-5

linear programming models 74-75

managers
    share in Material Incentives
        Fund 153-54
    tenure in post 145-48
Material Incentives Fund
    as percentage of income
        151-56
    definition 136-37
    distribution 143
    econometric evidence on its
        influence 156-60
    formation in eleventh FYP
        137-42
    profit share 23
Ministries
    annual plans and planning
        12-13
    classification 6
    importance in enterprise
        behaviour 111-12
    input allocation 32-33

Normed Net Production 16-17

optimum control models of
    enterprise 130-31

planned targets
    annual plans 14
    incentives and bonuses 142
prices
    formation 18

profit mark up 18, 20
profitability
    calculations of 20-21
    in simple enterprise models
        58-61
profits
    definition 19
    distribution and use 23
    gross/net 20-21
    investment finance 22-27
(Production) Development Fund 21
    output plan 14, 62-63, 68, 142

ratchet effect
    and bonuses 144
    as a price 132
    consequences on enterprises
        117, 129
    definitions 116-17

sales plan 142
Sociocultural and Housing Fund
    21, 143
supply curves of enterprises
    56-7

tautness
    causes 82-84
    definition 82
    effects on effort 84-85,
        130-1
    effects on performance
        102-5
    empirical evidence on its
        overall effects 98-105
technology (new) 150
Techprofinplan 14-15

uncertainty
    input allocation 97-98
    tautness 83, 91, 104-5

wages 137, 162

X-inefficiency 102-4